Moose–cellania

Moose–cellania

A Collection of All Things Moose

Bill Silliker Jr.
Walter S. Griggs Jr.

Down East Books
Camden/Maine

Printed at Versa Press, Inc., East Peoria, Illinois

6   5   4   3   2   1

ISBN 0-89272-668-7

Down East Books
Camden, Maine
A division of Down East Enterprise,
publishers of *Down East* magazine.
Book orders: 800-766-1670
www.downeastbooks.com

Library of Congress Control Number: 2004109063

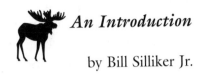

An Introduction

by Bill Silliker Jr.

One day an e-mail from another moose lover stood out from the rest of the herd. The writer had all four of my books on moose—*Maine Moose Watcher's Guide, Moose Watcher's Handbook, Moose: Giant of the Northern Forest,* and last but not least, *Uses for Mooses and Other Silly Observations.* While that flattered, what really intrigued me was his statement that he had been collecting moose trivia for years and had a large file of information about moose that went way beyond biology. And he had a question: Would I consider teaming up with him to do a book project?

Curiosity made me grab a telephone and call Walter Griggs. After we exchanged initial pleasantries, Walter said something I'll never forget: "My wife thinks I'm crazy—I've been collecting stuff about moose for years. I have boxes of it. But I have this thing about moose."

I knew exactly what Walter meant. The world seems divided into two camps: those who love moose, and those who don't really know them yet. And all the ones who love moose seem to "have a thing for them."

So I took Walter up on his challenge and approached the folks at Down East Books about the idea. And with a creative editor's suggestion, this book emerged.

Walter provided most of the research and compiled the information from his "boxes of stuff." I provided most of the moose photographs, items on moose biology, and some moose factoids from my own collection to round things out.

As a reader, all you have to provide is your own sense of wonder for all things moose. Enjoy.

— The Mooseman

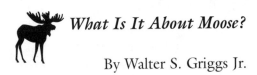

What Is It About Moose?

By Walter S. Griggs Jr.

There is something about moose that captivates me. Indeed, there is something about moose that makes me think that, at times, I am really a moose masquerading as a human being. However, I know I am not a moose, because my wife and daughter constantly tell me that I am human.

I need this reassurance in order not to start munching leaves or preening my dewlap. If I am not a moose, I constantly wonder why I have this "connection" with moose. I frequently ask myself, "What is it about moose that I find so fascinating?" And, this question is answered whenever I see a moose in its natural habitat. By looking at a moose, I feel the strength of a regal animal, whose curious configuration exudes the power of a creature that seems to be at peace with itself and with its world.

The moose is content because it seems to accept itself as it was created and not how it might have been created. Although it might look somewhat unusual in appearance, the moose is impressive because it is so unusual. In some ways, the moose seems like a combination of a diverse group of animals. Indeed, it is the horse-like head, bucket-like nose, mule-like ears, shovel-like antlers, foghorn-like voice, beard-like dewlap, camel-like hump, deer-like legs, horse-like body, and rope-like tail that make the moose so appealing, so captivating, so interesting.

Yet, there is more to a moose than its appearance. There has always been a special bond between humans and moose, since they have shared the North American continent with each other for thousands of years. And by looking at a moose, I can almost feel this sense of history. Native Americans respected the moose and called them "moos"; the black-robed French Jesuits wrote about the moose and called them "original"; explorers were mystified by the moose and called them "moose"; and today we look at moose and call them magnificent.

Across the years, artists have painted the moose, photographers have carefully selected f-stops to photograph the moose, and writers have tried to capture the essence of the moose in their prose and poetry. But you cannot fully capture the moose on paper or canvas. You must do something more.

Have you ever looked straight into the eyes of a moose? If you have, then you will realize that there is something all-knowing about this animal. There is something in those eyes that lets all moose-lovers know that a moose understands our confusion about his appearance and welcomes our kinship and respect. When you gaze into the eyes of a moose, you will connect with the spirit of God's Monarchs of the

Northern Forest and, like me, you will be captivated by the spiritual and mysterious qualities of the moose.

— The Dean of Moose

This book is dedicated to my late co-author, Bill Silliker Jr. When I first met Bill, I immediately thought of a moose; now when I see a moose, I immediately remember Bill.

I also want to acknowledge the support of my wife, Frances, and my daughter, Cara, without whose help this book would never have been completed.

— Walter Griggs

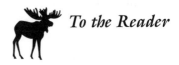 ## *To the Reader*

"Moose-cellania" is a new word, but this book requires a new word since the English language lacks an appropriate term to describe it. The etymology of this word can be traced to the fact that the moose appears to be an animal composed of miscellaneous parts and this book is composed of miscellaneous entries to describe the moose and its relationship to society. Therefore, it seems appropriate to take the word "moose" and the word "miscellaneous" and combine them to create a new word.

Because the moose is an unusual animal, it also requires a unique book format. Just as a moose has a large head and tapers down to a small tail, this book introduces each section with a broad overview of a moose-related topic and then tapers down to individual entries.

Moose lovers can choose to read this book from cover to cover. Or the passionate moose-person can read individual sections while waiting at a moose-crossing sign, with camera in hand, hoping for a moose to cross the road. Regardless of how you use this book, it is hoped that you will see the moose as a remnant of a world that is slipping away and as a reminder of a time when many humans depended on the moose for their survival in the New World. Perhaps by reading this book, you will join the herd of moose-people who can look into the eyes of a moose and see a magnificent manifestation of God's creativity.

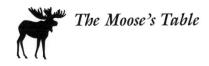 *The Moose's Table*

Understanding Moose Biology and Behavior

Many humans research their ancestors. They believe it is important to have a relative who landed with the first settlers at Jamestown, Virginia, or to be related to someone who sailed on the *Mayflower*. Humans are frequently zealous in researching their family trees unless, or until, they discover an ancestor who was hanged from a sturdy oak.

Although moose do not go to libraries to peruse family records, they do have ancestors; and it is important to have an understanding of these ancestors and of how the moose fits into the deer family. Just as humans can take pride in having sailed the stormy Atlantic to come to the New World, moose can take equal pride in having walked on dry land across the Bering Strait as they emigrated from Siberia to Alaska. However, there is a fundamental question that must be answered about this emigrating moose: How did a moose get to be a moose?

Like the current human models, moose have evolved

over a long period of time. It was more than forty million years ago that the distant ancestors of the first moose lived in North America. And moose scholars believe that the ancestors of the current moose first walked the Earth more than two million years ago. During this long period of evolution, early moose, like early humans, took some bizarre forms. Frequently, their antlers grew to enormous proportions atop their oddly-shaped heads. Today's moose, like today's humans, seem to be a vast improvement over their ancient relatives.

Another way to understand moose is to examine the way they are classified by biologists. The scientific community has an elaborate classification system for all creatures, both great and small. The classifications go from the general to the specific. As might be expected, the moose is first classified as an animal, but this is of little help in identifying a moose except to suggest that it is not a rock or a tree. To narrow it down, the moose is further classified as a *Mammalia,* which is still a very, very large family group; but at least it establishes the fact that the moose is not a fish or a bird. The moose is a member of the order *Artiodactyla,* which includes animals with two or four paired toes. This classification includes such diverse creatures as pigs, camels, cattle, and deer. The moose's closest relatives are in the family *Cervidae,* which includes animals with bony antlers that are shed and renewed. Such animals include the musk deer, caribou, tufted deer, hog deer, swamp deer, fallow deer, red deer, white-tailed deer, roe deer, and the moose. The moose is specifically classified with the genus and species *Alces alces*, but there are several species of moose in both Europe and North America that have their own specific classifications. It should be noted that if the members of the family *Cervidae* had a picnic, the moose would be the biggest one in attendance.

But there is more to a moose than its evolution and its classification by biologists. Moose are unforgettable animals. Once you see a moose, you will never forget it. They look as if they were put together by government bureaucrats using spare parts from other animals. These "spare part" creatures live in the northern climates in both the Old and New Worlds. Moose are vegetarians and their large size enables them to munch the tops of trees. In spite of their size, moose are fast runners, can easily move through dense woods, and are good swimmers. Bull moose are relatively passive except when their minds turn to thoughts of love and their antlers are lowered against other like-minded bulls. And a human moose-lover should NEVER get between a cow moose and her calves, unless he or she wants to be on the losing side in a modern-day version of the Battle of Armageddon.

The information in this section will increase one's knowledge of the moose's ancestors, its evolution, and its behavior.

Adam and Eve of Moose: One of the first known moose-like creatures was the stag moose or *Cervalces scotti*. A possible prehistoric ancestor of our modern moose, it earned the name stag moose because it had the palmated antlers associated with a moose, while its head was more like that of an elk. The stag moose's lifestyle probably compared to that of the modern moose.

Other early moose-like creatures include the *Alces gallicus*, which, except for its larger skeleton, closely resembles a modern moose. "Very long-beamed, small-palmated antlers" characterized it. Another early moose-like creature was *Alces latifrons* or *Libralces latifrons*. It had many of the characteristics of a modern moose.

Our present moose, called *Alces alces*, probably evolved in Eurasia and migrated to North America across the Bering Land Bridge. Scholars, like human genealogists, are still trying to determine the exact family tree of the moose. And it's interesting to note that while moose and moose-like fossils indicate a presence in North America for at least 150,000 years, the great expansion of moose across the northern tier of the United States and Canada has largely come only in the last 10,000 years, with the retreat of the last great glacier.

Agitated Moose: One that is nervous, startled, scared, or just plain mad. Actually, dogs get mad—moose get angry.

A really angry moose strikes out with its hoofs, sometimes rearing back as a horse does. Wise moose watchers also watch moose body language: ears dropped alongside the head, an angry glare, a flared mane, or bristled hair along the spine all indicate agitation.

Bull moose also toss their heads around and then drop their racks to display their antlers in a challenging statement. This is not a good time for a moose aficionado to make a moose grunt call!

Antler Growth: Moose antlers grow anew every year, regardless of how large they become. Starting as soft tissue that grows from the pedicles—two small, flat basal patches that lie forward of the ears on the male moose—the antlers become hardened by late summer.

The antlers of larger, more mature bulls grow rapidly. The "rack" of an adult bull in his prime looks fairly impressive by June of each year, despite its being covered still with "velvet," the blood-vessel-laden tissue that supplies antler growth from late winter to late summer. The antlers calcify and the bull moose sheds his velvet by the end of August, after it dries up and is no longer needed.

Moose bulls grow antlers to impress cow moose with their healthy genes and to scare off or fight with rivals for the mating rights to a cow or cows in their range. Moose drop their antlers each winter, as they are no longer needed after the fall mating season, or rut.

The average adult bull moose grows more than 40 pounds of antler in less than half a year. The Eastern moose and the Northwestern moose subspecies—which differ only in cranial details—grow their antlers larger than their Yellowstone region cousins but smaller than their Alaskan ones.

The 55-inch spread of an Eastern moose is considered large, although some have exceeded 65 inches. That's enough to carry around the woods while cruising cows, don't you think?

Alaskan bulls not only typically grow wider spreads, but also heavier antlers, with average weights in the 50-pound range.

Antlers: Moose antlers have frequently been the center of attention in some of the world's best-known residences. King Henry VIII had difficulty in keeping his wives, but had no difficulty in keeping moose antlers in the Horn Room in his residence in Hampton Court. Not to be outdone, President Theodore Roosevelt had moose antlers on display in the White House. If moose antlers could only talk, what a story they could tell.

At the Speed of Moose: Not all that fast normally: moose don't run without a reason. But when something scares them or they want to chase off a threat, moose make use of their long legs and can cover ground at an amazing pace. Several reliable sources have clocked moose at 35 miles per hour—faster than any human can run—with the possible exception of a human being chased by a bull moose.

Bad Hair Day: Actually a several-months-long event for moose, as they begin to shed their worn winter coats as early as March each year. The molt lasts into June, when they begin to grow new guard hairs that give them a clean, brown look by the fall and provide protection from the rigors of the coming winter.

Barren Cow: A childless moose cow—or perhaps one that is child-free, depending on how a moose looks at it. Raising a moose calf requires a lot of energy! Actually, while the existence of an adult cow that cannot produce a calf is quite unusual in the moose world, in any given year, only about half of the adult cows will give birth.

Brainworm: The common name given to a nervous system affliction, caused by a parasite carried by white-tailed deer that impairs and eventually kills moose. While it has no apparent affect on deer, this parasitic roundworm—*Parelaphostrongylus tenuis*—leads to a nervous system collapse, paralysis, and death for both moose and caribou.

Bull: What you should call a male moose. In September and October, you might also call him "Sir."

Calf: Moose babies—called calves—are about three feet long and three feet tall when born. Weights range from about 20 pounds to as much as 35 pounds—perhaps even more. Only mother moose knows for sure.

Calls of Moose: Moose make a variety of sounds to communicate with each other. Cows talk to their calves with a selection of grunts that all seem to have a meaning. The calves respond differently to grunts made at different times or for different reasons. While they might all sound alike to a moose watcher, nuances of moose pronunciation may give the commands different connotations as the calves appear to follow them obediently.

Moose calves make their own set of sounds, mostly either nagging "I'm hungry" or "But Mom . . ." squeaks, whines, or grunts.

During the rut, cow moose make a long wailing sound when in estrus that phonetically might go like this: "uunnnnweeeaaaagghhhoouuughhh." You get the idea?

Bulls cruise for a cow during the rut while intermittently making a distinctive grunt, something that sounds like "oouunnhh." They'll often patrol the edge of a clearing or pond, grunting every five seconds or so.

Outside the rut, mature bulls seem content to stay silent.

Cellular Moose: In Sweden, moose are tracked by being fitted with a phone with a global positioning device. One can only speculate what might happen if someone dials a wrong number and a moose answers with "*hejsan*" (a Swedish greeting).

Census of Moose: The total population estimated for North American moose has averaged just under a million moose for all jurisdictions with "countable" moose populations in recent years. While less certain, due to the lack of information from some regions, a conservative estimate of Old World moose tops that. As many as 1,500,000 moose, perhaps even 2,000,000, might roam the northern forests and taiga from the Baltic to Kamchatka in any given year.

Chew Cud: Something moose do a lot. As a ruminant—an animal that chews its food more than once—with a four-chambered stomach, moose depend on this to derive maximum energy from the plants on which they thrive. One study documented that moose spend about 40 percent of the day chewing their cuds—that's a lot of regurgitating!

That same study also found that the moose actively ate food another 40 percent of the day and slept 18 to 20 percent of it. Simple math says that a moose doesn't have much time left to do anything but eat and sleep—not a bad life, when one thinks about it.

Climbing Tree: A tree that lends itself to climbing in an emergency—one with lower limbs that provide a ready escape route should a moose watcher have a close encounter of the wrong kind with either a mad cow or a raging bull.

It does pay to have a climbing tree—or at least one you could step behind to block the possible charge of an angry moose—handy during the rut in particular. Keeping a respectful distance from a moose calf generally avoids the problem of an unpleasant encounter with a mother moose.

Cow: What you should call a female moose.

Darwin Award Candidates: A couple of researchers, who, in order to study the moose in Yellowstone National Park, put on moose costumes so they could get closer to the real thing. On one memorable occasion, *People* magazine reported that they were almost too successful. Detecting the imposters, the "moose lowered its ears, dropped its head, and the hair on its nape stood up." All of these are bad signs if one is a researcher in a moose costume too close to the real thing! Quickly, the researchers jumped out of their moose skins and scrambled to safety. One can only imagine what the moose thought.

Dewclaws: Two little "toes" on the rear of a moose's foot.

Dewlap: Not a word from a 1950s song lyric, but the name of a moose body part—the strange looking, hair-covered fleshy thing that hangs beneath the chin of both male and female moose. The dewlap is more substantial, with more surface area, on the bull moose. Some researchers believe that it serves as a visual indicator of sex and age, while others think that it might serve to spread odors of pheromones—sexual stimulants—during the moose rut. Only the moose know for sure. Also called a bell.

Domesticated Moose: Many efforts have been made to domesticate the moose. Easily domesticated, moose have carried messengers, pulled carts, pulled sleighs, raced horses, worked as draft animals, and become pets. And, there is a picture of Theodore Roosevelt riding a moose. But things are not what they seem. The picture is a clever composite and not the real thing. Of course, Theodore Roosevelt was not the first politician to pull a trick or two with his picture.

In 1910, Jack Carr of Alaska had two pet moose. He named the bull President William Howard Taft, and the cow was called Helen after the President's daughter. Carr was impressed by the intelligence of the twin moose and seemed to enjoy having them as pets. He also commented on what he called their "natural instinct." It seems that the moose could tell if a person liked animals. Carr wrote: "If any person goes near them who is fond of animals, they (the moose) will stand still and let them (the people) pet them and seem to like it; but if any person does not care for wild animals or pets, they will snort and back away." Perhaps with some training, moose could be taught to detect criminals and other assorted goons. Perhaps one day there could be a Moose Force to assist the police force.

Droppings: The real thing. A study revealed that the average moose produces 380 nuggets per day, or more than 11,000 per month, or more that 100,000 per year.

Since Alaska has 174,000 moose, that means a total of 17.4 billion nuggets per year, or enough for each person on earth to have four nuggets. There are also available numerous recipes called "moose droppings," which are edible. The trick is knowing the difference.

Environmental Concerns: Although the future of the moose seems secure, there was a time when its survival was in jeopardy because of excessive hunting and the destruction of its habitat.

Concerns for this magnificent animal have motivated some passionate prose on behalf of the moose. The Earl of Dunravern wrote:

> Poor *Cervus alces* [moose], your ungainly form has an old time look about it; your very appearance seems out of keeping with the present day. The smoke of the chimney, the sound of the axe are surely though slowly encroaching on your wild domain. The atmosphere of civilization is death to you, and in spite of your exquisitely keen senses of smell and hearing you too will soon have to be placed in the category of things that have been.

Henry Fairfield Osborne expressed a similar concern:

> Nature has been a million years in developing that wonderful animal [the moose] and man should not ruthlessly destroy it.

Perhaps all moose lovers should reflect on these thoughts when a community elects to sacrifice the natural habitat of a moose in order to build another shopping center.

Flying Moose: Pigs do not fly, but moose do. In order to establish a moose population in Michigan's Upper Peninsula, the Michigan Department of Natural Resources flew in more than thirty moose from Canada's Algonquin Provincial Park. The tranquilized moose hung in a sling beneath a helicopter. Later they were put in crates, loaded on a truck, taken to Michigan, and released. One can only wonder what a camper in Algonquin Park might have said upon looking into the sky and seeing a moose swinging under a helicopter.

Gestation: Exactly 234 days—sometimes. Actually, researchers over the years have documented a variety of times required to make a moose, anywhere from 216 to 248 days. But most seem to agree today that it takes about 234 days—give or take.

Guard Hairs: The heavy, air-filled long hairs of the moose coat that cover a moose's body and help protect it from the harsh cold it lives in much of the year. A moose also relies on its guard hairs to stay afloat: the hollow, air-filled center of these hairs helps make a moose somewhat buoyant. Guard hairs can range up to ten inches in length, but most are much shorter. Moose shed these every spring when they go through the annual molt.

Height of Moose: Moose reach their adult height at about two years of age. An average adult moose stands about seven feet tall—at the shoulder! The Alaskan subspecies—*Alces alces gigas*—is even taller, perhaps a foot taller on a really large moose.

Home Range: Not a cowboy's tune or a domestic cooking implement, but a term used to refer to the normal living area used by, and familiar to, animals of a given species. Food supply, seasonal variations in climate, the ability to get around, predator concerns, and other such influences probably impact the decision of a moose to determine its home range.

So what is the average home range for a moose? Only the moose know for sure. While many moose live in a range of about two to ten square miles most of their life, some studies find moose home ranges as wide as 36 square miles, and some even as large as 100 square miles.

Leg of Moose: About 40 inches long on a full-grown adult moose. It is easy to see why the moose can get a "leg up" on other animals.

Length of Moose: Moose measure from nine to ten feet in length, from the tip of the nose to their little tiny tail.

Lip Curl: Not the latest moose fashion craze (hey, some humans stick jewelry into theirs), but a behavior also known by the German word *flehmen*. It refers to the curling of the upper lip by a bull moose while holding his head high to get a better whiff of a cow's estrus scent during the rut. Bulls have a sensory organ in their palate that seems to serve as a strong receptor of the pheromones found in a willing female moose's urine.

Locked Antlers: Not something to prevent theft, but a serious predicament that bull moose occasionally get themselves into. Apparently the tines of their antlers interlock when the force of a thrust during battle spreads their antlers apart enough so that they become entangled. Stories of huge bulls succumbing to an agonizing death due to slow starvation, as they cannot unlock themselves from their adversary have been documented from Alaska to Maine.

Mad Cow: An angry mother—not a diseased one. Beware the mad mother moose, as she could chase you to run you off, or worse, rear up and kick you as a horse does. The front hooves of a protective mother moose make lethal weapons. While they will take the chance to leave, if pressed enough, moose mothers will aggressively defend their youngsters, especially during the tender months from birth in May to the fall.

Migratory Moose: Moose that make seasonal changes in their home range. For example, moose in Maine sometimes live their entire existence within a few miles of their birth site, while some change their range during winter by traveling to more open, windblown mountaintops, probably in search of more easily accessible food. Some moose in the Tetons do the reverse, as they descend from summer home ranges at higher elevations down to Jackson Hole, Wyoming, for the winter. Perhaps the many fine restaurants there also attract them?

Moose Count: While estimates of moose populations can vary from year to year, recent estimates from the 27 jurisdictions in North America with "countable" moose average close to one million animals each year.

Twelve of the Canadian Provinces/Territories host the bulk of the moose of North America: Alberta, British Columbia, Labrador, Manitoba, Newfoundland, New Brunswick, the Northwest Territories, Nova Scotia, Ontario, Quebec, Saskatchewan, and the Yukon.

Fifteen of the United States also have countable moose populations: Alaska, Colorado, Idaho, Maine, Minnesota, Montana, New Hampshire, New York (just barely—a handful live in the Adirondacks), North Dakota, Utah, Vermont, Washington, Wisconsin, and Wyoming.

Moose Counters: While those biologists and researchers who try to count moose use aerial surveys, infrared detectors, radio tracking, computer projections and the like, moose numbers are "guesstimates" at best. Counting any wild animal population is an art at best. Not even the moose know how many of them exist.

Moose Countries: Moose—also called elk in Europe and Asia, even though they are all moose at heart—today live in Canada, China, the Czech Republic, Denmark, Estonia, Finland, Lithuania, Norway, Manchuria, Poland, Russia, Siberia, Slovakia, Sweden, and the United States.

Moose Country: Any place with good moose habitat, specifically northern boreal forest. Most biologists agree that seven subspecies of moose inhabit the moose range of the northern hemisphere, four in North America and three in Europe and Asia, where they are also called elk. Moose have extended their range back into what once was moose country in recent years, with sightings in forested parts of Massachusetts and even Connecticut. Fossil remains suggest that North American moose country once extended as far south as Oklahoma and South Carolina. Imagine seeing a moose in Dixie? But those who live in Hawaii can rest assured that there is no chance one will move into their neighborhood.

Moose Cuisine: Moose thrive on aquatic vegetation, the buds and twig ends of a variety of trees, leaves, bark stripped off some deciduous trees, and other plant materials. Strictly herbivores, they eat as much as 50 pounds of wet weight daily in the summer, when pondweed and similar such vegetation is available, and perhaps 35 pounds or so of dry winter forage.

Moose Hump: The large hunk of muscle over the shoulders that serves to help hold the long neck and nose of the moose upright. This hump seems more pronounced on bull moose, as they also have as much as 60 or more pounds of antler headgear to carry around for part of the year. Those who might take this for a hump similar to that of the camel, and mistakenly think that these two species share genes or at least ancestors, would be wrong. Moose belong to the deer family and are, in fact, the largest deer in the world.

Moose Jaw: A normal moose has a total of 32 teeth, mostly molars and premolars. Moose have no upper canines or incisors, and few lower ones. Because they are herbivores, they don't need to rip meat.

Moose Milk Scientific studies suggest that moose milk, which, of course, comes from a moose, has certain curative powers. Moose milk is easy to obtain from a moose since the "moose milker" can stand up while milking the moose and does not need the traditional milking stool.

Moose Repellent: There are people who do not like for moose to eat the trees and plants in their gardens. Of course, the moose are only "doing what comes naturally," but some people just do not understand. For such thoughtless individuals, there are a variety of commercial repellents on the market. However, there are several natural repellents that have been used with success. These include hanging bear skin in the yard or bars of soap on the trees.

Moose Tail: A joke that God played on the big beasts, as they have nothing with which to swat flies. The average moose tail averages a couple of inches at best—on average.

Moose Tracks: An adult moose makes a somewhat oval-shaped imprint about six inches long and four inches wide. Larger moose leave larger footprints—duhhhh. And while a moose has four "toes," the two large front hoofs show most often, while the rear "dew claws" show only in softer surfaces as the moose sinks in more. The spreading of these four toes enables a moose to wade through bogs and mud with greater ease. Which way did the moose go? The way the toes are pointing—duhhh again. Okay, here's a hint: moose toes narrow more towards the front.

Most Moose in North America: The claim for this distinction goes to British Columbia, with an estimated 175,000 moose. Newfoundland comes in second, with 111,000 moose.

In the United States, Alaska has the most moose, with an estimated population that runs in the 150,000 range. Maine places a distant second, with an estimated 29,000 moose. But Maine might have claim to the highest density of moose in the United States, as in some good moose habitat areas, particularly where forestry has led to regenerating new growth, moose have thrived in recent years.

Most Moose in the World: Sweden beats them all, with between 200,000 and 250,000 moose (European elk) currently estimated to be living there each winter. Where do they go in the summer? Why, the Riviera, of course.

Actually, moose winter populations are considered by

some to be a more accurate indication of true numbers because the estimate at that time of year typically follows the harvesting of moose, includes the calves of the year that have survived their first fall, and because sampling for projections is somewhat easier once the leaves have fallen.

Mother Moose: Moose cows can mate at sixteen months of age. Those yearlings that do mate usually give birth to a single calf. The more mature cow moose often give birth to twins. On average, one could say that moose give birth to twins about one third of the time. Some even have triplets.

Mother of All Moose: A cow moose photographed with four calves following her on June 28, 2002, by Bill Silliker Jr., on a pond that is part of The Nature Conservancy's Katahdin Forest Project in Maine. The four moose calves swimming along behind the cow that evening had been seen and reported as a family group for about two weeks previously. This photograph has some moose researchers pulling their dewlaps. Did this moose cow give birth to all four calves? Only the moose knows for sure.

Mousomodai: Another name for the dewlap, or bell, according to naturalist Ernest Thompson Seton: "The Indians call the pendant *mousomodai* meaning literally 'moose bottle'."

Naturalized Moose: There have been several instances

where moose have been introduced into an area they had not formally occupied.

Two examples are as follows:

> Ten moose were captured in Saskatchewan, transported by ship across the Pacific Ocean, and introduced into New Zealand in 1907. The population peaked in at around 70 moose. They are now probably extinct.

> In 1878 and 1904 moose were successfully moved from the North American mainland to Newfoundland. Moose are now well established in Newfoundland, with recent population estimates of over 100,000 moose!

The fact that there were moose in New Zealand might suggest the following poem:

> Only in New Zealand can you see
> A moose munching lunch with a kiwi

Neonatal Predation: This fancy phrase describes the likelihood that something will eat a moose calf.

Nuggets: Moose scat. Found in the woods in prodigious piles, moose nuggets are oblong and typically about $\frac{1}{2}$ an inch long. Entrepreneurs in moose country fashion them into necklaces, earrings, bracelets, and a host of highly sought-after gifts. Co-author Walter Griggs once kept a jar of moose nuggets on his desk to remind him of the moose.

Unfortunately, someone ate a few and he had to remove them. He thinks they were mistaken for peanut M&Ms.

Old Moose: A bull moose in the wild would be lucky to make it to fifteen years. In fact, in one study of a non-hunted moose population, the oldest bull died before making it to his sixteenth birthday, while some cow moose made it to their twentieth birthday. The average life span of most moose was just under eight years for the cows, seven years for the bulls. Moose die from predation, accidents, disease, starvation, hunting, or just plain old age.

Old World Moose: The elk—or moose—of Europe, Russia, and China. These cousins of the North American moose, distant by location only, are basically the same animal—the majestic moose. Canadian biologist Dr. Randolph Peterson described three subspecies in his ground-breaking work *North American Moose,* published in 1955:

> *Alces alces alces:* the European moose, found in Czechoslovakia, Denmark, Estonia, Finland, Lithuania, Norway, Poland, Russia, and Sweden.

> *Alces alces cameloides:* the Manchurian moose, found in the Amur/Ussuri Region, Manchuria, and Mongolia.

> *Alces alces pfizenmayeri:* the Siberian moose found in Russia and Siberia. These largest of the

Old World moose most resemble the moose of Alaska.

Pedicle: A bony protrusion just in front of each ear of a bull moose, from which antler growth develops.

Predators of Moose: Bears, wolves, and humans are the greatest natural enemies of the moose. It is somewhat difficult to change bears and wolves, but humans are another matter. Humans must be careful in driving through moose areas and obey all game laws.

Punch of Moose: When threatened, moose kick with their front legs. A kicking moose is an awesome sight unless you are the target of his hoofs.

Raging Bull: One you really want to allow its space. Male moose typically lose a lot of inhibitions and change their usual calm demeanor as the pressure of hormones drives them to distraction during the fall mating season, or rut. Beginning in about mid-September and running till mid-October, the rut finds bull moose on the prowl for an amorous cow moose almost constantly. Research shows that mature bulls stop eating for days as they cruise for cows, grunting and thrashing the woods with their big racks of antlers. It's definitely not the time of year to get in the way of one!

Record Rack: Not a place to store disks or files, but a really big set of moose antlers. Despite the fact that antlers grow from scratch every year, some racks of antlers span over 6 feet in width, and can weigh more than 60 pounds. For example, an Alaskan hunter shot a bull moose in October 2002 that carried a rack 74 3/8 inches wide!

Salt Lick: Pretty much what it sounds like—a place to lick salt. Moose crave sodium and other minerals at certain times of year, especially in the spring as they—depending on the moose—need milk to nurture young or grow new antlers. While they seek out natural mineral deposits when possible, moose will also lick the salt treatments used on roads during winter, right off the surface of a road, sometimes laying down to do so!

Spring and early-summer vegetation and muddy spots alongside roads throughout moose country also provide salt sources, as the deicing treatment flushes to the roadsides and attracts many moose. Drivers in moose country should always be on the alert for moose in the road, especially during the winter and the spring salt-lick seasons.

Scaredy-moose: While a bull moose in the rut can be a force of nature to behold—and to beware—most moose have a calm, almost timid behavior. They often sneak through the woods as quiet as a mouse. But when afraid of something, their behavior changes dramatically. As Randolph L. Peterson wrote: "When badly frightened there is probably no animal in North America that makes more noise crashing headlong through dense brush."

Sense of Moose: While some people claim moose to be "dumb" animals, they only show their own ignorance by doing so. Perhaps they haven't encountered many moose, or if they have, they've not been paying attention. Given a chance, moose show a lot of good sense, and become very wary animals if heavily pressured by predators or hunting.

Otherwise, they typically behave with a quiet, gentle demeanor with the exceptions of mother moose guarding their calves and bull moose during the short rut in the fall. Thoreau wrote of two cow moose that his party hunted in *The Maine Woods:* "They made me think of great frightened rabbits, with their long ears and half-inquisitive, half-frightened looks; the true denizens of the forest."

Senses of Moose: While moose have poor eyesight, they possess excellent hearing and an acute sense of smell. They make use of their hearing and scenting capabilities to warn of danger or simply to keep track of what's going on around them. Once they hear or smell something, if not frightened by it, they will often stare inquisitively at it, as if trying to determine its purpose.

Moose mothers also identify their offspring—and other moose—by their unique scent. The sight of a mother and her calf bonding by touching noses offers the moose watcher one of nature's most tender moments.

Sign of Moose: Moose fans looking for a moose should look for the signs moose leave as clues: deer-like tracks that extend 6 inches in length; nipped buds and tree-branch ends that are too high for a deer; scraped bark where a bull rubbed his antlers; beds, or depressions, in grassy areas big enough for a moose to have curled up for a nap; and prodigious piles of pellets, reminiscent of large chocolate-covered peanuts.

Subspecies of North American Moose: *Alces* is the taxonomic classification for the moose. *Alces* means elk in Latin. While that may seem incorrect, it reflects the fact that the Old World cousins of the North American moose, which include three subspecies living in Europe and Asia, are called elk. The early European settlers in North America followed Native Americans in their designation of this similar animal as moose, which roughly means "twig eater."

Most biologists agree that several subspecies of moose live across North America:

> *Alces alces americana,* the Canadian or eastern moose. The second largest of the North American moose subspecies, it ranges across the northern tier of states from the Great Lakes to the Atlantic coast.

> *Alces alces shirasi,* or the Wyoming moose. Generally considered the smallest North American moose.

Alces alces andersoni, or the northwestern moose, found from northern Michigan and Minnesota westward to central British Columbia and northward into the Yukon and the Northwest Territories.

Alces alces gigas, or Alaskan/Yukon or tundra moose. The largest of the North American moose, and among the largest moose in the world.

Swimming Moose: Moose swim well, and, with the extra buoyancy provided from their hollow guard hairs, don't have to struggle as much as we humans do to stay afloat. A moose can swim as fast as a really good paddler can paddle a canoe, according to Kim Morris, a moose-researcher from Maine who was trying to fix a collar around the neck of one from the bow of that same canoe. A less scientific estimate says that a moose can swim at least 5 miles an hour.

And they have been documented swimming miles out of sight of shore in Lake Superior and even in the ocean, where one source (*Moose*, text by Valerius Geist; photography by Michael Francis; Voyageur Press, 1999) states that swimming moose have been attacked by killer whales.

Why does a moose swim? To get to the other side, of course. Even in the ocean? Only the moose knows for sure.

Talking to Moose: For many reasons, humans enjoy talking to moose. There are a number of ways to do this.

Native Americans made various moose-like sounds into a horn fashioned from birch or cedar bark to "talk to the moose." Contemporary "moose linguists" can use one of the wide variety of moose calls on the market to discuss current events with a moose.

It is also possible to make a moose call by punching a hole in the bottom of a tin can and pulling a long, wet, shoe-lace back and forth through the hole. It is helpful to hold the can under your arm while pulling the shoelace. Of course, it is helpful to know a little "moose language."

Various moose scholars have tried to translate "moose language" into English:

Samuel Merrill, in *The Moose Book,* suggests the following "moose sounds": "Mwar" or "Oo-oo-aw" or "O-oh-ah." He also suggests playing the Swedish National Anthem on a violin or trying to imitate the sound of a ship's foghorn.

Edward E. Flint, in *Forest and Stream,* provides some helpful calls in his moose writings. He wrote that saying "Oh-oh oh-oh" or "Moo-waugh-yuh" would convey an appropriate message to a moose.

Bill Silliker, the Mooseman, suggests "weeaahhhoowww" as "moose speak."

And Walter Griggs, a Virginian, has yelled "Y'all come" with mixed results from the moose, but with strange looks from humans.

In talking to a moose, it is necessary to be careful since

your voice inflection or a mispronounced "Oo-oo-aw" could insult a bull moose and produce unfortunate results.

Undercoat: Not a preservative to prevent rust, but a most important layer of short hairs that protect a moose from the elements. These wooly hairs average one inch in length and cover most of a moose, providing protection throughout the year.

Wallow: A scraped earth pit that a bull moose digs and urinates into during the rut, which apparently serves as an aphrodisiac. The bull then lies in the pungent-smelling mud and rolls around. If he's tending a cow, she will jump in as well. Co-author Bill Silliker has seen a cow smack a bull with a front hoof to get him to leave the wallow so that she could take her turn at it. Some researchers believe that scent covers the dewlap during wallowing, and as it dangles from a moose's chin, it thus helps spread the scent.

White Moose: A white moose is not an albino, but rather a very rare color variant. It has a dark nose and eyelids, and has black flecks amidst its white hair.

Willow: More important than the wallow, the willow marks a predominant food source for moose all across North America. Moose watchers looking for moose would do well to seek out large patches of willows when in moose country.

Yearling Moose: A year-old moose. You knew that? Did you also know that the yearling moose holds a special place in the moose world, that of the lost and bewildered teenager? Mother moose run their calves off just before their first birthday, making it a very difficult time for the poor bewildered creatures. After following mother for about every move since birth, the yearling must now make its own decisions, avoid danger, defend itself, and find its place in the moose world—not an easy thing to do at this tender age.

Yearling moose often wander the woods and show up on roads in moose country. Drivers should go slow—especially after dark—whenever in moose country, but they should be especially aware that yearlings might step out into the roadway from mid-May into June as they wander about looking for their place in the world. Driving with care can avoid that place being as your hood ornament.

 *Artistic Moose*

Frequently, when a person looks at the painting of the Mona Lisa, they are overcome by powerful emotions. This mysterious woman evokes feelings of awe and mystery. Such feelings often surface when a person looks at a picture of the moose.

There have been many artists who have tried to capture the moose's image in artistic compositions. Thousands of years ago, Native Americans painted moose on rocks. Although the renderings are crude and frequently display a long, dangling dewlap, they are definitely of a moose. Perhaps the artist most closely associated with the moose is Carl Rungius, who loved to paint the "moose among the spruce." Looking at a moose painted by Rungius, one can see the power of the moose and the skill of the artist. Besides Rungius, there are many other artists, both past and present, who were captivated by the moose and sought to preserve a special moment in an artistic medium. This section will give other examples of the "moose and art."

Artist of Moose: Carl Rungius, a native of Germany and the son of a minister, studied art in spite of his parents' wishes that he enter the ministry. In 1894, he came to the United States and became one of America's outstanding wildlife painters. Carl Rungius painted many pictures of moose. In fact, he is known as the "Rembrandt of the moose." When asked his favorite subject, he responded that it was "the moose in the spruce."

Centennial Moose: Sculpted by Gerald Balciar, "Centennial Moose" is a magnificent bronze moose that is in residence in Mooseheart, Illinois. Dedicated in 1988, this statue commemorates the one hundredth anniversary of the Loyal Order of Moose.

Mark Trail: Created by Ed Dodd and now written by Jack Elrod, Mark Trail is far more than a cartoon character—he is America's best known preservationist of woods, waters, and wildlife. His message to "reduce carelessness and abusive activity such as littering, vandalism, theft, and wildlife poaching" has reached millions of Americans.

Jack Elrod, a United States Navy veteran of World War II, has been associated with *Mark Trail* since 1950. When Ed Dodd retired in 1978, Jack took over the cartoon series completely. Jack Elrod is able to capture the mystique of the moose in his cartoons. A Georgia native, Jack's work has certainly put "moose on my mind." The recipient of many awards and honors for his work, Jack Elrod has made all Americans aware of the natural beauty of their nation and the need to preserve it for future generations.

Melville Moose: Pittsfield, Massachusetts, has a program called Artscape. The program's purpose is to bring public art to downtown Pittsfield. One such piece of art is a magnificent standing moose statue by Glenn Hines of Hammond, Maine. The statue stands 9 ½ feet tall and weighs 4,000 pounds. But there is more to the story. A contest was held to name the moose, and the community named it Melville. Why Melville? Well, Herman Melville, the author of *Moby Dick*, wrote his famous novel while living in Pittsfield. And in the book, Melville has Captain Ahab saying of Moby Dick that "he shouted with a terrific, loud animal sound, like that of a heart-stricken moose . . ." Therefore, it seems most appropriate to name a moose statue Melville.

Queen of Moose: Charles Pachter, a well-known Canadian artist, has painted a number of portraits of Queen Elizabeth II with a moose. In addition, the artist has put Prince Charles on canvas admiring the moose. The Prince's plumed hat is tilted in deference to the animal king of Canada. Although the Royal Family seems to appreciate the moose, they have not started singing "God Save the Moose."

Statuesque Moose: Many statues of moose decorate North America. The largest appears to be the statue of Mac Moose in Moose Jaw, Saskatchewan, Canada. This colossal statue stands 32 feet tall and weighs 10 tons. Another mega-moose statue, Maximillion or Max Moose in Dryden, Ontario, serves as a fitting "Moosecot for the community."

Other moose statues include Morris the Moose in Goobies, Newfoundland, and Howley the Moose in Deer Lake, Newfoundland. In addition to the many moose statues in Canada, the town of Greenville, Maine, enjoys a statue of a flying moose.

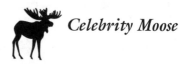 *Celebrity Moose*

Most moose do not seek fame; they prefer to live in anonymity among the spruces. But, alas, fame has claimed some members of the herd and their names have become household words. These moose have become celebrities and much has been done to promote the popularity of the large quiet animal. Listed among the stars are Bullwinkle, the cartoon moose; Rutt and Tuke from the movie *Brother Bear*; and the Moosel.

This section will focus primarily on moose who have sacrificed the peace of the boreal forest in order to please their adoring public, but it will also include some non-moose celebrities.

Baseball players named or nicknamed Moose: Several Major League Baseball players have shared the moniker of the moose.

> Bob Moose was a pitcher for the Pittsburgh Pirates. Born in 1947, he died in 1976.

> Bryan Edmund Haas, a Major League pitcher, was called Moose. Born in Baltimore in 1956, he

pitched for both Milwaukee and Oakland. He retired in 1987.

George Livingston Earnshaw, a Major League pitcher from 1928 to 1936, was nicknamed Moose or Big Moose.

William Joseph Skowron, known as Moose, was an infielder from 1954 until 1967. Born in 1930 in Chicago, he played in seven World Series for the New York Yankees and one for the Los Angeles Dodgers.

Bullwinkle J. Moose: The most famous of all moose, Bullwinkle was born and raised in Frostbite Falls, Minnesota. He played football for and is a graduate of Wossamotta U. Bullwinkle is governor of Moosylvania. His constant companion is Rocket J. Squirrel.

Disney Moose Movies include:

The Moose Hunt, released on May 3, 1931, featured a moose and was the first cartoon in which Pluto was known by name.

Moose Hunters, released on February 20, 1937, told the story of how Goofy and Donald Duck dressed up like a female moose to lure a bull moose as their victim. Unfortunately for Goofy and Donald, they were chased by a bull moose and had to run for their lives.

Morris, the Midget Moose was released on

November 24, 1950. Morris was a midget-size moose with mammoth antlers who became the laughing stock of moosedom until he met Balsam, a large moose with minuscule antlers. The two outcast moose teamed up and, with Morris riding on Balsam, they defeated the leader of the herd.

Brother Bear was released in 2003. The movie starred two moose brothers named Rutt and Tuke.

Donny Moose: Given by members of Moose International, Donny is a cuddly, plush moose with white hair. This special moose serves as a caregiver for people living in retirement communities or in nursing homes. The gift of a Donny Moose lets the elderly know that people still care about them. And because he has some white hair, this moose feels right at home with senior citizens.

General Bullmoose: Created in 1953 by cartoonist Al Capp for the *Li'l Abner* comic strip. The general was a capitalist who lived by the motto, "What's good for General Bullmoose is good by the U.S.A.!"

**Jackson, Benjamin Clarence,
a.k.a. "Bull Moose" Jackson:** Benjamin Clarence Jackson, a saxophonist and vocalist, was nicknamed Bull Moose. His 1947 recording "I Love You, Yes I Do" became the first

rhythm and blues single to sell a million copies. Bull Moose, who became a cult hero, died in 1988.

Krause, Edward "Moose": Coach Krause was an outstanding coach and All-American athlete for the University of Notre Dame.

Manner Moose: The name of the moose created to teach children good manners. Manner has been described as a "comical-looking moose with suspenders, a bow tie, and flowing dreadlocks for antlers."

Medic Moose: The Calgary, Alberta, Canada, Emergency Medical Services gives a stuffed miniature Medic Moose mascot to children treated by paramedics.

Mister Moose: A character on the *Captain Kangaroo* show staring Bob Keeshan. From 1955 until 1968, Mr. Moose dropped ping-pong balls on the Captain's head and told him knock-knock jokes.

Moosylvania: a small island in the Lake of the Woods, Minnesota. Bullwinkle J. Moose is governor of Moosylvania, but doesn't live there. The United States and Canada dispute ownership of Moosylvania: neither country wants to claim it, each stating that the island belongs to the other.

Morty Moose: Morty may be the most watched moose

of all times. Why? Morty was the moose that walked down the street in the opening scene in the early 1990s television program *Northern Exposure*. Reportedly, bananas were used to encourage him to walk down the street. Morty, who went to moose heaven at the age of five, was a member of a moose herd maintained at Washington State University.

Seymour of Anchorage: A costumed moose used to promote Anchorage, Alaska. Seymour appeared in Seoul, South Korea, in a failed effort to get the 1992 Olympics to come to Anchorage. It was reported that other delegations "don't have any moose dancing for them."

Soap Opera Moose: As a result of a contest, the parrot on the soap opera *One Life to Live* was named Moose. Reportedly, the parrot said, "Loose as a moose" on the show.

Tommy Moose: This plush toy is donated by Moose lodges and chapters to their local fire and police departments, which need something to give to young children in crisis situations. For young children, there is nothing more calming than a plush animal, and no plush animal is more soothing than Tommy Moose!

Wuzzles: *The Wuzzles* was a cartoon series created by the Disney Studio. Each Wuzzle was a combination of two different animals. For example, the hippopotamus and rabbit were combined to create the Hoppopotamus. Moose lovers will quickly see that the Moosel is a combination of the moose and the seal; Moosel has the head of a moose and the body of a seal. Although *The Wuzzles* was not a television success, it did end up in Federal Court in a case of alleged copyright infringement. In writing his opinion, the judge wrote: "In the Land of Wuz lived the Wuzzles. We don't know where Wuz was . . . But we were told we could get there if we snuzzle a Wuzzle."

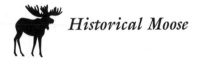 *Historical Moose*

Many historians have recorded the role of moose in history. In 400 B.C.E., Herodotus, one of the earliest historians of the western world, commented on "enormous animals" in his writings. In the first century C.E., the Roman scholar Pliny the Elder wrote of "the elk [moose] which strongly resembles our steers, except that it is distinguished by the length of [the] ears and of the neck." Perhaps the moose's enormous size and unusual appearance have inspired historians to focus their research on the moose. Scholars have researched the writings of early naturalists, the Jesuit fathers, the early explorers of New France, and many others who have recorded their observations concerning the moose. Historians have also played a major role in preserving the oral traditions of the Native Americans. These records enable the contemporary reader to get a clearer understanding of what people thought about the moose and how the moose impacted the development of North America. History can be exciting; and no history is more exciting than that of the moose living among awestruck humans who were trying to comprehend their woodland neighbors.

This section has numerous examples of how historians have captured the moose's past and its hope for the future.

Big Moose Lake, New York: This lake in the Adirondack Mountains was the home of a steamer named *Big Moose*.

Bridge of Moose: The Bering land bridge that once extended from Siberia to Alaska's Seward Peninsula. During several periods of the Pleistocene Ice Ages, walking on the land bridge permitted the 55-mile passage without getting your feet wet. This bridge enabled both humans and moose to walk from Asia to North America on dry land. Once humans and moose reached the New World, they were trapped when the ocean covered up the land bridge.

Most researchers believe the moose arrived in the New World about ten thousand years ago, prior to the first humans. Unfortunately, the first moose-human contact is not recorded, but it must have been quite amazing for both man and moose.

Caesar's Moose: Julius Caesar wrote in *The Gallic War* that "there are also [animals] which are called elks [moose]." He continued: "They have legs without joints and ligatures; nor do they lie down for the purpose of rest. If they get tired, they just lean against a tree." While this, of course, is not accurate, it indicates that Caesar had some acquaintance with moose.

First Documented Mention
of Moose in North America:
Historians debate which European explorer was the first to meet a moose. Several possibilities exist. Jacques Cartier, who was seeking a northwest passage to Asia, explored the St. Lawrence Valley in 1535. Although there is speculation that he might have seen a moose, there is no definitive evidence that he did. Samuel Eliot Morrison wrote that in 1567, or possibly 1568, David Ingram, an English sailor, reported seeing on the Maine coast "a beast farre exceydinge an ox in bigness, with floppy ears like a blood hound and long hair." Was this a moose?

The founder of New France, Samuel de Champlain, might well have been the first European to use the word moose in the French language. In June of 1603 he wrote in French as follows: "*Il y a aussi plusieurs bestes sauuages, comme orignas. . .*" The English translation is as follows: "There are also many wild beasts, such as orignacs [moose], . . ." *Orignacs,* which is sometimes written as *orignal, orignac,* or *orignas,* is believed to be the Basque name for deer. It is speculated that the Basque fisherman who arrived very early in Eastern Canada used this word for moose. The modern French word for moose is *l'orignal*.

Marc Lescarbot, a lawyer, poet, and writer from Paris, spent some time in Acadia. On his 1609 map of Port Royal, Nova Scotia, Lescarbot showed the Moose River with a moose drawn near the water. Most scholars agree that this is the earliest existing picture of the American moose. Around the same time, he wrote the following: "But first let us speak of the Elk, which they [the Native Americans] call *Aptaptou*, and our Basques, *Orignacs.*" Around 1612, there is a reference in the *Jesuit Relation* that "in the neighborhood of Port Royal they took six *Grignaces.*" The word *Grignaces* is derived from the Basque word *orignacs*.

The first clear mention of the moose in the English language is by Sir Ferdinando Gorges in *Purchas' Pilgrimage.* The author wrote, "Captain Hanhgam sayled to the River of Sagadahoc [in] 1606. He relateth of their beasts . . .redde Deare, and beast bigger, called the Mus."

In a later edition of the work, published in 1625, the author wrote, "There is also a certaine Beast, that the Natives call a Mosse [moose] hee is as big bodied as an oxe."

The English adventurers continued to write of the moose in the following years. William Wood wrote a poetic account of the moose in 1634. The poem, entitled "New England Prospect," is as follows:

> The kingly Lyon, and the strong arm'd Beare
> The large lim'd Mooses, with the tripping Deare,
> Quill darting Porcupines, and Rackcoones bee,

Castelld in the hollow of an aged tree;
The skipping Squerrell, Rabbet, purblinde Hare,
Immured in the selfesame Castle are,
Least red-eyd Ferrets, wily Foxes should
Them undermine, if rampird but with mould.
The grim fac't Ounce, and ravenous howling Woolfe,
Whose meagre paunch suckes like a swallowing gulfe,
Blacke glistering Otters, and rich coated Bever,
The Civet sented Musquash smelling ever.

Thomas Morton in 1637 described the moose in prose when he wrote: "First, therefore I will speake of the Elke, which the Salvages call a Mose: It is a very large Deare, with a very faire head, and a broade palme, like the palme of a fallow Deares horne but much bigger, and is 6 footewide between the tipps, which grow curbing downwards: He is the bigness of a great horse."

There is still much speculation about the first recorded sighting of a moose by a European. The quest for an answer is in itself an exciting adventure.

Franklin's Moose: When he was a young boy, Benjamin Franklin wanted to see two moose in Boston that were waiting to be shipped to Queen Anne of England. A stranger paid the two pence required to let young Benjamin see them.

Perhaps this stranger's generosity led Benjamin Franklin to suggest that "a penny saved is a penny earned" when he years later wrote his famous proverbs.

Gladiator Moose: It is known that European "elk"—moose—probably from Norway, were used in the Roman Coliseum to fight in the bloodthirsty gladiatorial games. It is not known whether the moose fought other animals or gladiators. Although this sport is disgusting and totally inhumane, it is hoped that the moose was a fearsome combatant with its charging antlers and flying hoofs. And surely the moose said in its most fearsome call, *Morituri te salutant:* "Those who are about to die salute you."

God's Own Horses: Henry David Thoreau's appellation for the moose: "These are God's own horses, poor, timid creatures, that will run fast enough as soon as they smell you, though they are nine feet high."

Gold Moose: In 1936, a moose ate $30,000 worth of gold dust. Perhaps this moose is the only moose to drop "gold nuggets." One can only speculate what a prospector might have said if he thought he had discovered gold nuggets and they turned out to be moose nuggets.

Hudson's Bay Company: Chartered in 1670, Hudson's Bay Company has long been associated with the Canadian fur trade. The official description of the company's coat of arms stipulated that two elk—elk is the European name for moose—should support the company's shield.

For an artist to draw two elk (moose) holding the Hudson's Bay Company shield would appear to be a simple task. Unfortunately, the artist apparently drew two deer-like animals that only remotely resembled moose, and which were in fact the North American animal called elk! Fortunately, the official written description for a coat of arms takes precedent over an artist's rendering; thus, these elk are really moose at heart.

James, Frank: The brother of Jesse James was an ardent supporter of Theodore Roosevelt. To show his support, he called his cattle by yelling "Bull Moose."

Jefferson's Moose: French naturalist Georges-Louis Leclerc, Comte de Buffon contended that the life forms in Colonial America were inferior to those same life forms in Europe. Indeed, he wrote that the New World was a "land best suited for insects, reptiles, and feeble men." This assertion caused Thomas Jefferson, the United States minister to France but soon to be the President of the United States, to use the moose to defend the pride of Colonial America. Jefferson wrote that "the elk (moose) of Europe is two-thirds of the height of the American moose."

In addition, Jefferson asked the Governor of New Hampshire, John Sullivan, to obtain the skeleton of an American moose to be sent to France for de Buffon to study. After seeing the skeleton, de Buffon wrote to Jefferson: "I should have consulted you, sir, before publishing my natural history and then I should have been sure of my facts." Thus, Jefferson and the moose won an academic war against France.

Appropriately, moose antlers are prominently displayed at Monticello, Jefferson's Virginia home.

Jingle Bell Moose: Charles IX of Sweden used moose to pull his sleigh. Had this practice become popular, people would be singing: "Dashing through the snow, with a one-moose open sleigh."

Lincolnesque Moose: In an article in a 1940 issue of *Nature* magazine, Vernon Bailey wrote that the "moose is not a beautiful animal, but he has strength, character, individuality, and he stands out among our native mammals somewhat as Abraham Lincoln stands out among and above the leaders of men."

Madam Moose: George Washington's dog. United States presidents have had a wide variety of pets, ranging from John Quincy Adams' alligator to a wallaby owned by Calvin Coolidge. Other presidential pets have included pigeons, goats, and lizards. But probably because of its size, no president has had a moose in residence in the White House—yet.

Magoon, George, a Poacher of Moose: At one point in its history, the Roman Catholic Church suggested that a beaver might well be a fish. George Magoon of Maine tried a variation on this idea by suggesting that a moose was really a cow. However, Magoon's motives were not religious.

To avoid being convicted of moose poaching in 1910, Magoon's lawyer argued that the meat Magoon had in his possession was the meat of a cow and not the meat of a moose. This line of argument prevailed and Magoon was acquitted. A newspaper editorial asked the question: "Will someone who knows all about it please step forward and tell us how to distinguish moose meat from 'bull' meat?" And strange as it seems, this defense was "no bull."

Moose, Charles: The Montgomery County, Maryland, police chief who successfully led the task force that captured the snipers who had terrorized the I-95 corridor in October 2002. Chief Moose resigned in 2003 to write a book about this experience.

Moose Cure: It was believed that a moose suffering from epilepsy could cure itself by scratching its ear with the left hind foot. Believing that this remedy would work on humans, there was a demand for the left hind feet of moose for human use. Thankfully for all concerned, this remedy is no longer in use.

Moose Factory, Ontario: At first glance, this Canadian city appears to be a place that manufactures moose. When asked about the name, the locals respond by saying that "we get the moose knees from Moosoness, Ontario, and the jaws from Moose Jaw, Saskatchewan." Less exciting is the truth, which is that "moose" comes from the nearby Moose River and "factory" comes from the word "factor," which is the term used by a fur-trading company to designate the person who heads the trading post. Since the Hudson's Bay Company trading post was on the Moose River and was headed by a "factor," the community became known as Moose Factory.

Moose, Pvt. Frederick V.: Known to his friends as Virgie, he served in the 52nd Georgia Regiment during the Civil War. Private Moose has been included in this work to represent all members of the Family Moose who served with valor in the Confederate Army during the late unpleasantness.

Moose Jaw: The city of Moose Jaw, Saskatchewan, has a rich heritage. It has been a winter encampment for the First Nation, a fur-trading camp, and a divisional point on the Canadian Pacific Railroad. Located in the heart of Canada's wheat belt, it was granted city status in 1903 and has continued to thrive as "the Friendly City" on the Canadian prairie. But there is more to the story of Moose Jaw. Because of a direct rail route from Chicago and the existence of underground tunnels beneath Moose Jaw, Al Capone and his Chicago goons frequented the city. Like rats, they slithered through the tunnels to avoid being apprehended and to enjoy the various underground entertainment opportunities that were available in this city with the intriguing name.

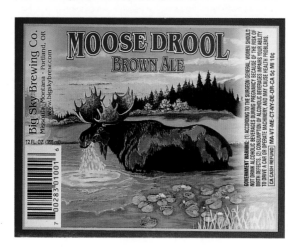

MOOSE DROOL
BROWN ALE

Big Sky Brewing Co.
Missoula, Montana · Portland, OR
www.bigskybrew.com

12 FL. OZ. (355 ml)

7 00283 01001 6

GOVERNMENT WARNING: (1) ACCORDING TO THE SURGEON GENERAL, WOMEN SHOULD NOT DRINK ALCOHOLIC BEVERAGES DURING PREGNANCY BECAUSE OF THE RISK OF BIRTH DEFECTS. (2) CONSUMPTION OF ALCOHOLIC BEVERAGES IMPAIRS YOUR ABILITY TO DRIVE A CAR OR OPERATE MACHINERY, AND MAY CAUSE HEALTH PROBLEMS.

CA CASH REFUND MA-VT-ME-CT-NY-DE-OR-CA 5¢ MI 10¢

MOOSEHEAD
BREWERIES LIMITED

Insignia for Canadian naval vessel, HMCS *Moose*.

A ferocious moose pursuing a terrified Hitler was the gun shield adornment of the corvette HMCS *Moose Jaw*.

Right: Moose migration from Canada to Michigan via helicopter.

Flying moose

Energized moose

Above: A stock certificate for Maine's Bangor and Aroostook Railroad and a schedule for the Belfast & Moosehead Lake Railroad.

Left: The mascot of the Alaska Railroad.

Below: The Bull Moose locomotive of the New Haven, CT, Railroad.

Though moose cows generally have only one or two calves at a time, Bill Silliker captured the lower photograph of a cow followed by four calves.

Moose in the Minnesota Game Exhibit
at the 1904 World's Fair.

Badge of the International
Order of Foresters.

From the Coast Guard to the Air Force to police and fire departments, moose are representatives of numerous agencies and organizations.

USCGC SUNDEW (WLB-404)

THE SUPERIOR ONE

DULUTH, MN

Many Canadian military insignia feature a similar design

NE-KAH-NE-TAH

THE ALGONQUIN REGIMENT

CANADA

CANADIAN SQUADRON

242

ROYAL AIR FORCE

TOUJOURS PRÊT

SQUADRON

ROYAL CANADIAN AIR FORCE

MOOSA ASWALTA

TRIBAL POLICE

KONGIGANAK ALASKA

FACTORY

MOOSE ISLAND

FIRE & RESCUE

"Moose" in American Sign Language.

The U.S. Navy ship *Moosbrugger* features a moose on its cap and a moose head, with antlers, in its ready room.

The moose bird, A.K.A. Canada jay or Gray jay.

The Loyal Order of Moose is an international fraternal organization that directs charities to help children and the aged.

Country Moose

City Moose

Medic Moose

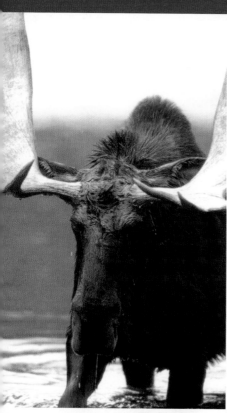

Wuzzle

Tommy and Donny Moose

Olympic moose

Bullrock the Moose, Dixfield, Maine

Even a moose can't resist
the opportunity to take a
good photograph.

A number of explanations for the name Moose Jaw exist. Some people believe that because of the "warm breezes" that blow through the area, the First Nation members called it *Moosegraw*, meaning "warm breezes," which is translated "moose jaw." Another theory is that the city was named Moose Jaw because an English lord's cart broke down and the man repaired it with a moose jaw. The First Nation's word for "the place where the white man mended the cart with the jawbone of the moose" is *Moosoochapiskun*. Another explanation is that the name comes from the shape of the nearby Moose Jaw River, which has a turn shaped like the jawbone of a moose. The First Nation word for the "river shaped like the jaw of a moose" is *Moosoochapiskanissippi*. Apparently no one has suggested that someone found a moose in a jar and exclaimed, "There is a moose jar!" Regardless of the origin of the name, Moose Jaw is a lovely city with an interesting past and an exciting future.

Moose Music: Early European hunters of "elk"—moose—frequently took a violinist on moose hunts. The violinist would play a selection, the moose would hear it, leave its forest home, and be dispatched by the waiting hunter.

On at least one memorable occasion, the moose, hearing the violin played for the would-be hunter, analyzed the situation, lowered his antlers into attack mode, charged the violinist and hunter, and forced them to scamper like squirrels up a nearby tree. Perhaps not a big fan of Moozart?

Moose Pass: A community in Alaska where, according to local lore, a moose blocked a dog team carrying the mail in 1903. Apparently "neither snow nor rain nor heat nor gloom of night" can stop the mail, but the post office wisely did not include the moose in this mandate.

Moose Peak Light: Authorized by President John Quincy Adams, the Moose Peak Lighthouse still serves as an aid to navigation. The closest town to it is Jonesport, Maine.

Mooseless Expedition: Did the Lewis and Clark Expedition come up mooseless?

The Corps of Discovery, led by captains Meriwether Lewis and William Clark (technically a second lieutenant, "promoted" by Lewis and President Jefferson for the expedition), served as the first United States overland expedition to the Pacific Coast and back, from 1804 to 1806. While they documented and described the wildlife encountered in thousands of miles of travel from St. Louis, Missouri, to the Oregon coast and back, neither of the two leaders recorded any personal contacts with moose in either of their journals.

But several of the expedition members did make reference to them. For example, on May 10, 1805, Sergeant John Ordway wrote: "Saw several moose deer which was [sic] much larger than the common deer and the first we have seen."

Although it is not certain, Lewis and Clark may have sent the moose antlers that are on display at Monticello to Thomas Jefferson.

Place Names: Many geographical features in both the United States and Canada are named for moose. Madison Grant wrote that moose "shrink back before the most advanced outpost of civilization, and soon vanish altogether, leaving behind the names of lakes, rivers, and mountains as the only evidence of their existence." Although the moose might have left an area, their name remains as a reminder of a time when the mighty moose walked where homes and shopping centers now stand.

In the United States, there are more than 600 places named for moose or parts of a moose. These places include: Moose's Tooth, Moosehead, and Mooseheart in Alaska; Moosehorn in Connecticut; Moose Jaw in Idaho; Moose Neck in Maine; and Moose Ear in Wisconsin. Some names are especially interesting, such as Moose Can Gully, Idaho, and Mooselookmeguntic, Maine, the longest hyphenless place name in the United States. *Mooselookmeguntic* means "where the hunters watch the moose at night." Another unusual place name was Moosecajik, which means "moose's rump," the ancient Indian name of Cape Rosier on Penobscot Bay in Maine.

In Canada, there are almost 700 places with moose in their names. Bodies of water include the Moose River and Moose Creek in Ontario, Moose Bath Pond in British Columbia, and Moose Ear Pond in Newfoundland. Places named for parts of the moose include Moose Jaw in Saskatchewan, Moosehorn in Manitoba, and Moose Hide

Hills in the Yukon Territory. There is also Moose Mountain, Saskatchewan, Moose Land, Nova Scotia, and Moose Factory, Ontario.

From the Atlantic to the Pacific and from the north of Canada to the south of the United States, there are more than 1,300 places named in honor of the moose. Such recognition is a lasting testimony to the influence of the moose on the landscape of North America.

Shiras, III, George: A United States Congressman from Pennsylvania, devout conservationist, and wildlife photographer, Shiras perfected the art of night-light photography and was the first photographer to use the technique to photograph moose. In the July 1906 issue of *National Geographic,* there is a picture of a moose photographed by Shiras at night. Under the picture is the following caption: "When the flashlight was fired the moose charged the canoe [on which the camera was mounted], knocking the camera overboard." But, the negative was saved. In his honor, a subspecies of moose was named for him. The Shiras moose (also known as the Wyoming moose) is the smallest subspecies of the North American moose.

Social Control Moose: Animals are frequently used as a means of controlling children through fear. For example, parents might tell a misbehaving child that if he does not clean his room, a moose will munch on him. Studies show that, although the bear is generally the most popular animal with which to threaten children, moose are also used for this purpose. It has been suggested that its size and large antlers make it look fearsome to children.

Stanley, Frederick Arthur: Lord Stanley, the Governor General of Canada from 1888 to 1893. He crossed Canada by railroad to promote western settlement and the locomotive had a large pair of moose antlers over its headlight. Although best known for his antlered locomotive, he is also known for the Stanley Cup, which is named in his honor. The National Hockey League gives it to the champion hockey team each year.

**United States Custom Services
and the Border Crashing Moose:** The United States Customs Service is charged with protecting the borders of the United States. Although not generally known, the Customs Service has an X Sector that responds to calls reporting suspicious activities such as drug smuggling or narcotics trafficking.

The men and women of X Sector are known as Sector Enforcement Specialists (SES) and are trained to respond to every conceivable inquiry. But they were shocked when an inspector on the Alaska-Canada border yelled over the phone, "A moose just ran the port—please advise." This incident has become legendary in the Customs Service.

Unrequited Love: In this era of political correctness, no one would make fun of a person with impaired vision. However, such compassion does not apply to moose. Moose have poor vision, and sometimes that apparently interferes with their love life. In 1986, a love-struck bull moose called Josh courted a female bovine named Jessica at a farm in Shrewsbury, Vermont. For more than 76 days, the amorous moose tried to woo the cow, but without success. Almost 50,000 curious humans came to see the star-crossed lovers. Perhaps this bull moose needed glasses? Whatever the case, this episode adds a moose meaning to the phrase " 'Tis better to have loved and lost than never to have loved at all."

World's Fair Moose: The World's Columbian Exposition held in Chicago in 1893 featured several moose sculptures by Alexander P. Proctor. A pair of moose was located near the ornate administration building. And there were other moose on display. A moose called The Great Moose was in the Shoe and Leather Building. The states of Kansas, Maine, and Michigan all featured stuffed moose in their displays. Since many scholars believe that *Chicago* was the Native American word for "skunk," it was certainly a positive decision to place such a magnificent animal as the moose in such an unfortunately named city.

The moose was also featured at the St. Louis World's Fair held in 1904. In the Forestry, Fish, and Game Building, the state of Minnesota displayed a mounted moose to represent Minnesota wildlife. Surely someone sang this song:

> "Meet me in St. Louis, Louis,
> Meet me at the MOOSE."

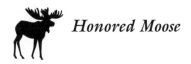 *Honored Moose*

The moose is a distinguished animal. Its very appearance suggests that the moose is not some oversized deer, but rather a noble creature that deserves respect. It is not surprising that this magnificent animal has been honored by lending its name to a vast array of diverse things, including geographical locations, mascots, and nicknames.

Excellent examples of honored moose are the hockey teams nicknamed "moose." The mental image of a raging bull moose charging down the ice to score a goal is an awesome manifestation of power. This section will show that there are many other examples of how the moose has been honored by those who truly respect its powerful image.

Beer Moose: Even though some jurisdictions make it illegal for a moose to consume beer, several beers are named for moose and are enjoyed by humans. These moose beers include:

> Dixie White Moose Beer: Dixie Brewing Company, New Orleans, Louisiana. This beer has been described as a sweet, vanilla-flavored brew.

Moose Drool Beer: Big Sky Brewing Company, Missoula, Montana. Moose Drool is chocolate brown in color and has a creamy texture. It is the best-selling beer brewed in Montana. Apparently, it makes a moose drool for more.

Moosehead Beer: Located in New Brunswick, Canada, Moosehead Breweries traces its roots to 1867, making it Canada's oldest independent brewery. To represent the company's commitment to high quality and excellence, the brewery chose the majestic Canadian moose as its symbol of strength and stature.

It should be noted that Stoopid Moose Beer is no longer brewed. It is now known as Temecula Valley Beer and Ale Works, Inc. The name was changed after Moosehead Brewery of Canada brought legal proceedings. It was reported that a Moosehead Brewery spokesperson said, "Mooseheads and the moose name we defend very vigorously."

Bertha Moose: Bertha, the mascot of the College of Forestry and Conservation at the University of Montana, is the only female moose with well-developed antlers. Frequently, the law students who are members of the Moose Appropriations Team, steal Bertha. To retrieve the moose, the College of Forestry has the Forester's Armed Response Team. Although this story might not pass "the smell test," it does show how important the moose is to university students.

Caboose Moose: To transport troops during World War II, the Pullman Company built the "moose caboose." Some of these cars have been converted into cabins.

Drinks of Moose: The moose is associated with a number of drinks that are sometimes noted for their high alcohol content:

> Moose Blood: During French Colonial times in Canada, wine frequently spoiled on long ocean voyages from Europe. To make it more palatable, the wine was mixed with alcohol and spices and then heated. The resulting beverage was called "moose blood."

> Moose Milk: When the British took control of Canada, they substituted whiskey for wine as the basic ingredient in moose blood. The whiskey was mixed with goat's milk, nutmeg, and cinnamon, resulting in a potent mixture called moose milk. Contemporary "moose milk" uses whisky or rum and spices along with a combination of eggnog and ice cream.

A word of caution with moose milk. A gun cleaner called "moose milk" exists, which is a combination of oil and water. And there is the real moose milk, which is high in nutritional value but not available at your local dairy counter. Since these products lack any known governmental regulations, they should be consumed or used with great care.

Flying Moose: A paraphrase of the opening lines of the old *Superman* television show might read as follows:

> Look!
> Up in the sky!
> It's a bird!
> It's a plane!
> No, it's a flying moose!

And yes, there really is a flying moose. A moose is pictured on the 20-foot tail of a Frontier Airlines Boeing 737-300. Certainly a flying moose makes an unusual sight as it speeds through "the wild blue yonder."

Golden Moose: The name of the award given by the School of Management and Economic University in Växjö, Sweden, to foreign exchange students in the field of business administration.

Hard Time Moose: The State of Minnesota maintains a level-three, medium-security institution at Moose Lake. It is not known if any errant moose have ever been incarcerated there.

Independent Order of Foresters: Members of this order wear a badge that features a moose head. Founded in 1874 in Newark, New Jersey, the Order is one of the world's largest financial services organizations. The organization "operates within the framework of members helping members."

Kampinoski National Park: The symbol of this park in Poland is the elk (moose), a popular animal in the region. The elk (moose) was introduced into the region in 1951.

Mascots: Mascots include the following well-known moose:

>Calvin the Moose: the "official moose" of the radio station Moose Country 102 in Fargo, North Dakota. Calvin, who walks on two legs, makes public appearances to promote the station.

>Juice the Moose: Mascot of the Midland, Texas, Rock Hounds baseball team. The team is affiliated with the Oakland Athletics.

>Mariner Moose: Signed as the mascot of the Seattle Mariners baseball team in 1990. In addition to being the team's mascot, he is also a spokesmoose for the great Northwest.

>Mick E. Moose: Official mascot of the Manitoba Moose hockey team. Mick began his career as the mascot of the Minnesota Moose Hockey Team. However, it seems that Mick had immigration problems and had to return to Canada. Without their mascot, the Minnesota team

faltered and moved to Manitoba to catch up with Mick, who became their mascot again. Go Moose!!!!

Yale University Moose: Yale has a special relationship with the moose. Two Yale mascots are as follows: Pierson College has a Moose Room so named for the stuffed moose residing therein. Ezra Stiles College has a moose with a unique history. When Bart Giamatti resigned as master of Ezra Stile College, he asked for a joke gift and he was presented a stuffed moose head. Giamatti advised his successor in solemn tones to "take care of my moose."

Monkey Moose: Moose love to eat bananas when they are in captivity. Could they possibly have some monkey genes in their family tree?

Moose Dog: A beagle named Moose served as a contraband dog with the United States Army in Germany. His handler would order, "Moose, show them what you can do!" And Moose would respond by finding hidden drugs. This dog served his nation in the highest tradition of the United States Army and in many ways was an "Army of One."

Moose Dropping Festival: Talkeetna, Alaska's, annual festival features moose droppings in ways that include the following:

Moose Droppings Toss—a game where players toss moose droppings at a target.

Numbered Moose Droppings—dropped from a weather balloon, with the moose dropping falling closest to a mark on the ground being declared the winner. To avoid any misunderstanding, moose are not dropped, only their droppings.

Moose in the City: 325 life-size sculptures of moose were placed in Toronto, Ontario, in 2000. Mayor Mel Lastman wrote: "We've got tourist moose, chocolate moose, dragon moose, hockey moose, golden moose, bride and groom moose, and maple leaf moose." In a press release it was reported "herds of majestic moose have taken over Toronto's street corners, squares, and boulevards in an extraordinary outdoor art event."

Moose International: A private fraternal organization composed of about one million five hundred thousand men and women members in the United States, Canada, England, Wales, and Bermuda. The family fraternity consists of two units: the Loyal Order of Moose and the Women of the Moose. The fraternity supports Mooseheart, a home for children in Illinois who are in need of a caring environment, and Moosehaven, a retirement community in Florida for aging Moose members and their spouses. In addition, the

Moose members support local charities and the needy in their own communities.

Members of the Order are frequently asked why they are called moose. One of their early enrollment ceremonies answered the question as follows: "The moose takes only what he needs, nothing more . . . yet for his great size and strength he lives in peace with other creatures. The moose uses his size and power not to dominate but to protect, not to spoil but to preserve. He is a fierce protector, a loyal companion, and a generous provider who brings comfort and security to those within his defending circle." Moose members have included Presidents Theodore Roosevelt, Warren G. Harding, Franklin D. Roosevelt, and Harry S. Truman.

Moose Run Golf Course: Located in Fort Richardson, Alaska, it is the oldest 18-hole golf course in the state. As golfers are playing the course, they could quite likely see moose munching food. Because of the number of moose in the area, it would seem appropriate to call a "birdie" a "moosey" when playing on this course.

Moose Mainea Festival: Held in Greenville, Maine, at the foot of Moosehead Lake from mid-May to mid-June each year. Activities—beside watching moose—include the Tour de Moose Bike Event, the Moose River Canoe Race, and the Moosehead Rowing Regatta. The Mooseterpiece Craft Fair, Moosehead Flycasting Tournament, Moose Tales, and the Moose Photo Contest mark the climax of the festival. The Visitor's Center in Greenville keeps a record of all the moose sightings, which sometimes total more than a hundred per day.

Murphy Moose: A real flying moose—an airplane manufactured by Murphy Aircraft Manufacturing, Limited. This airborne moose can operate with wheels, floats, or skis. One example of this plane is painted yellow and white with a bull moose on its nose, which makes it a magnificent "flying moose."

Nearly a Moose: How can an animal be nearly a moose? It is a moose, or it is not a moose? The answer is that Nearly a Moose is not a moose at all. Rather, Nearly a Moose is the name of the horse that won the Hewlett-Packard Galway Plate in Galway, Ireland, in 2003.

North Country Moose Festival: Held each summer in Colebrook, New Hampshire, this celebration of moose features a variety of activities, including a Mock Moose Parade, guided Moose Tours, Moose Watcher's Breakfast, "Christmoose" Crafts Fair, and many other moose-related activities.

Public Service Moose: Many police and fire departments feature a moose on their badges and patches. Surely the sight of a moose on a uniform inspires confidence and courage to those in harm's way, as well as to those seeking to rescue them. And a speeding driver would surely wilt when stopped by a police officer wearing a moose on his or her uniform.

Racing Moose: Although they have never run in the Kentucky Derby, moose have had a long association with racing. Moose have been trained to pull sulkies as if they were racehorses. Therefore, it is not surprising that The Outdoor Channel sponsors a car in the NASCAR races that features a moose painted on the side.

Of course, true moose lovers might object to having a moose associated with a sport that evolved from bootleggers running moonshine down "Thunder Road." But it can also be said that the fastest moose on land is the moose painted on a racecar. The Outdoor Channel also sponsors a Bandolero Car that can be described as a "turnkey spec-series racer designed for drivers as young as eight years old and the young-at-heart at any age." Appropriately, The Outdoor Channel's moose-bedecked Bandolero Car is fueled by "moose juice" to propel it around the track.

Railroad Moose: Even though trains and moose do not have good working relationships, many railroads have nicknamed their most powerful locomotives after the moose.

> The Union Pacific Railroad named a powerful articulated locomotive Bull Moose. This locomotive helped push long freight trains over the

mountains and perhaps snorted somewhat like a bull moose.

The New York, New Haven & Hartford Railroad named at least two locomotives after the moose. A consolidation steam locomotive was called Bull Moose. Although powerful, these locomotives required a lot of physical strength on the part of the engine crew to operate. It can be suggested that it takes a real moose of an engineer to run the Bull Moose locomotive.

The New Haven EP 5 class of electric locomotives was also call the Moose. Other names for this picturesque electric locomotive included: Jet and Dim Lights.

The Seattle Renton and Southern Railway in the state of Washington had an inter-urban car that was called Bull Moose because of its large size compared to conventional streetcars.

Even the British have remembered the moose. They call their Class 20 diesel locomotive the Moose because of the shape of the locomotive's nose.

In addition to naming locomotives after the moose, railroads have used the moose in both their corporate names and their official logos. Maine, for example, has The Belfast & Moosehead Lake Railroad. Although this railroad is very short, it has pride. Pat Shaw, one of the conductors, said, "This here railroad might not be as long as the Canadian Pacific, but by gory, she's just as wide." Appropriately, the

Belfast & Moosehead Lake features a moose in its company logo.

The Intercolonial Railway, which was organized to link the Canadian Maritime Provinces to the St. Lawrence River, had a moose in the center of its corporate symbol. Although the Belfast & Moosehead Lake Railroad is still operating, the Canadian National has absorbed the Intercolonial. It can surely be said that the moose are still working on the railroad.

Railroaded Moose: Railroads have long played a major role in the development of both the United States and Canada. Although railroads have been nation builders, they have not been a blessing for the moose. Moose and railroads have always been a bad combination. There are many instances of moose being hit by trains, with disastrous results for the moose and sometimes for the train.

The lonesome sound of a train whistle has captured the minds of writers and poets through the ages. However, these mournful, eerie, wailing sounds cause problems for the moose. A newspaper captured this dilemma in a brief poem: "What seems to be a she-moose lowing / may be just a diesel blowing: Don't confuse romance with an eastbound freight." To avoid this "fatal attraction," engineers sometimes refrain from blowing their locomotives' horns in moose country so the bull moose will not confuse a screaming horn with a cow moose in waiting.

The Algoma Central Railway of Canada used another

approach. It changed the sound of its diesel horns to a sound that the moose found disgusting.

Sled Dogs Named Moose: Although records are not complete, a number of sled dogs have been named Moose. Perhaps there is some risk in this since if the dog's owner called, "Mush, Moose," he might get his dog to run, or he might start a moose on a rampage.

Space Moose: The proposed name for the Canadian-produced space arm was "moose." A newspaper reported that the name "moose" is the essence of big, strong, and Canadian."

Stock Certificate Moose: The Bangor & Aroostook Railroad in Maine featured a bull moose on its stock certificates. Other stock certificates which feature a moose include the following: Menominee Motor Truck Company, Northern Co-operative Society, Adventure Consolidated Copper Company, Detroit–Cleveland Warehouse and Realty Company, Pennsylvania, Poughkeepsie and Boston Railroad Company, and Purity Bottling Works Limited. These stocks give new meaning to the term "bull market."

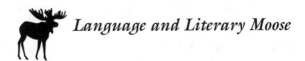 *Language and Literary Moose*

Since the publication of the King James Bible in 1611, the English language has assumed a richness that is beautiful to hear and exciting to read. In North America, this richness has been enhanced by the inclusion of many Native American words, including the word moose. The very sound of the word causes the image of a gigantic creature to form in a person's mind and suggests its native origins.

Using the word "moose" and reflecting on its image, many writers have written about the moose. Authors have tried to capture the moose in poetry and prose—both eloquently and otherwise. Charles C. Ward, in an 1878 copy of *Scribner's Monthly,* wrote: "[Presently] a magnificent moose came out into the open and walked quietly down to a pond . . . with his head erect and his broad antlers thrown back almost to his withers; his jet black skin, spotted white by the chequered sunlight, shone as glossy as satin." In a poem entitled "Birch and Paddles," Charles C. D. Roberts wrote the following lines: "Have spied the antlered moose cropping the young green spruce."

In this section will be found other examples of how

writers have written about the moose as well as definitions of some moose-related words.

Acronyms: MOOSE has frequently been used as an acronym. Examples include the following:

Moose: Management of Organizational Skills Everyday

Moose: Method for Object-Oriented Software Engineering

Moose: Model-Based Object-Oriented Software Generation Environment

Moose: Model-Based Object-Oriented Systems Engineering

Moose: Move Out of Saigon Earliest (from the Vietnam War)

Moosemuss: Maneuver, objective, offensive, surprise economy of force, mass unity of command, simplicity, and security. (The basic principles of war from Karl von Clausewitz.)

Black Moose: The name some early settlers of Pennsylvania called the moose that they found there to distinguish them from the elk that once thrived there, which they called gray moose. According to fossil records, during the Pleistocene, moose ranged as far south as present-day South Carolina and Oklahoma, when the habitat at such places was different than it is today.

Bull Moose Party: A political party formed in 1911, the Progressive Party used the bull moose as its mascot. Its presidential candidate, Theodore Roosevelt, proclaimed himself as "strong as a bull moose." One of the party's campaign songs contained these lines: "The moose has left the wooded hill; his call rings through the land." Another campaign song ended with these lines: "With a red bandana waving up on high / He's for Bull Moose, do or die." Poetry also found a place in the campaign. Arthur Guiterman wrote these lines in support of the Bull Moose campaign:

> The Bull Moose is galloping over the world
> And he loudly refuses to do as he's told.
> He tosses his antlers and goes it alone;
> For he scorns all conventions—excepting his own.

Children's Books: Many children's books have been written about the moose. And this is understandable. Moose are fascinating creatures whose exploits and wanderings can create very interesting stories. Just as young children tend to get into bizarre situations, the same can be said of the moose. Some examples of "moose books" are:

> *Blue Moose* by Richard D. Lansing, Jr., is an exciting adventure tale for children. A blue moose is also featured in a book by Daniel Manus Pinkwater. In this book a blue moose engages in many interesting endeavors, including wandering into a restaurant and devouring many bowls of chowder. These humorous stories can be found in *Blue Moose* and *Return of the Moose*.

Bruce Moose is concerned with "what ifs." His unusual story is told in *Bruce Moose and the What–Ifs*, by Gary J. Oliver, H. Norman Wright, and Sharon Dahl.

Bub Moose is the title of a book by Carol Wallace, Bill Wallace, and John Steven Gurney. Bub is an inquisitive baby moose that is warned to stay away from humans, which is probably not a bad idea. Of course, one will have to read the story to see if Bub heeds the warning.

Deneki is a moose whose adventures are described in *Deneki: An Alaskan Moose*, by William D. Berry. Published in 1965, this book is considered a classic.

Elliot Moose lives in Canada and has many experiences, including baking a cake, taking a bath, and digging for treasure. The Elliot Moose books are written by Andrea Beck.

Honk, the moose, gets loose and wanders through a town. Although his adventures are humorous, they are based on a true event. The book was written by Phil Strong and is appropriately entitled, *Honk the Moose*.

Latouse is a moose with somewhat of an identity crisis. This intriguing problem is told in the book *Latouse My Moose*, by Robert Tallon.

Little Brother Moose is featured in a Native

American account of the adventures of a young moose that leaves his forest home for an adventure in the community. The book, entitled *Little Brother Moose,* is by James Kasperson and Karlyn Holman.

Manfred Moose (TM) is a globetrotting moose who flies to Hong Kong. If one is planning a trip by airplane, this book by Ron Irwin is an essential travel guide for both humans and moose.

Maynard, the moose is featured in a book written by Marybeth Baker. The title of the book is *The Adventures of Maynard and the Loon.*

Mickey, the moose, not Mickey Mouse, has many thrilling adventures in Yellowstone National Park. His adventures are reported in *Mickey Moose,* by Bob Reese.

Moody Moose seems to have a number of medical problems and is treated by the town physician in *Moody Moose Buttons,* by Richard Hefter.

Moosey Moose has an unusual need for a moose: he wants to wear long pants. Can you imagine a moose in long pants? The story of his dilemma is told in *Moose (Thingy Things),* by Christopher Raschka and Chris Raschka.

Morris Moose is the focus of a series of books by B. Wiseman. Morris does a number of exciting things, including going to the circus and attending school.

Mouse is not the typical name for a moose, but then what is a typical moose name? Mouse Moose and a young girl meet and the girl is fascinated by the moose's "big, funny horns that look like cauliflower . . ." The book is entitled *A Moose Called Mouse*, by Martine Murray.

Muscles is an appropriate name for a moose, given their strong muscles. Muscles is a bull moose whose story is told in a series of books by Douglas DeVries.

Orville Anderson Tarkington Moose is a young moose who becomes very sad and alarmed when he discovers his antlers are loose. You'll have to read *Antlers Forever*, by Frances Bloxam and Jim Sollers to find out how he handles this crisis.

Santa's moose plays a critical role in solving a major problem for Santa. The thrilling adventure is reported in the book *Santa's Moose*, by Syd Hoff and Sydney Hoff. When Santa needed a fog light he summoned Rudolph, but when he needed muscle power he called on Milton, the moose, to assist him.

Spruce Moose has a crisis. His antlers continue to grow, and grow, and grow. To find out how his dilemma is resolved, you will need to read *Spruce the Moose Cuts Loose*, by Sarah Stapler.

Thidwick is a moose with a kind heart whose antlers become home for many of his woodland neighbors. The legendary Dr. Seuss wrote of this kind moose in the book *Thidwick the Big-Hearted Moose.*

Too-Loose is an unusual moose in that he is made of chocolate. Such a moose certainly has a unique set of problems. This sweet story is told in *Too-Loose the Chocolate Moose,* by Stewart Moskowitz.

Toulouse, with a different spelling and not made of chocolate, is the story of a moose who goes on a picnic with his cat. This unusual relationship is recorded by Monique F. Rea in *The Original Story of Toulouse the Moose and His Friends.*

Dean of Moose: Co-author Walter Griggs, who collected and collated most of the historical and some of the hysterical material for this book. Before discovering moose, he appeared on "What's My Line" as a dog-license collector and on A&E's "The Love Chronicles" to discuss his book, *General John Pegram, CSA.* The United Daughters of the Confederacy awarded him the Jefferson Davis Medal for this biography.

Walter's real occupation as the Associate Dean of Undergraduate Studies for the School of Business at Virginia Commonwealth University provides him with an academic background that served him well as he researched the many facets of the moose to fulfill a lifelong fascination with these huge, hairy beasts.

Descriptions: Because they are unusual, many people have tried to describe a moose in words. The challenge is to describe an animal that is so magnificent it is difficult to describe and, at the same time, so unusual that it defies description. Some of these efforts are as follows:

> The moose is singularly grotesque and awkward to look at. Why should it stand so high at the shoulders? Why have so long a head? Why have no tail to speak of? for in my examination I overlooked it entirely. Naturalists say it is an inch and a half long.
>
> — Henry David Thoreau

> Moose are huge! They are the size of a draft horse and heavier than a Volkswagen. As a matter of fact, they look kind of like a Volkswagen on stilts.
>
> — Government of Northwest Territories

> The moose looks disproportioned and ungainly, a ragtag mix of a lot of things, none of them fully realized—the head is an early attempt at something equine; the slope of the back from butt up to shoulder hump suggesting a start on a giraffe, abandoned early, before the designer had the courage to take the design all the way.
>
> — Trudy Dittmar

> The long legs of [the moose], which, together with the short round body, the thick horizontal neck, rendered more disproportioned by its

heavy coating of hair, the long wattle which hangs like an old-fashioned purse from underneath the angles of the jaw, the shovel-like antlers, the small sinister eyes, the enormous ears, the apology for a tail, and the prodigiously long and ugly head, finished with a nose resembling a half-inflated football, make the moose perhaps the most ill-favored of the four-footed animals. That ungainly head is stuffed full of brains. Those prodigious ears are ever trimmed, like the windsails of an ocean steamer, to catch the lightest breath of the fickle wind, and to apprehend and determine the cause of the faintest sound, which may be borne upon it. [Its] awkward shambling trot, and crashing through the forest with a noise like a railroad train off the track, the startled animal fairly devours space with the speed of its flight.

— Henry P. Wells

The sight of moose among the spruces always gives an added charm—the consciousness of the presence of a noble form of wildlife. There is something mysterious about the moose—something evoking a sense of creatures of the long past. To see one skulking in remote wilderness depths arouses primitive emotions difficult to analyze.

— Charles Sheldon

The Moose or Elke is a Creature, or rather if you will a Monster of superfluity; a full-grown Moose is many times bigger than an English Oxe, their horns . . . very big (and branch out into palms), the tips thereof are sometimes found to be two fathom asunder, (a fathom is six feet from the tip of one finger to the tip of the other, that is four cubits) and in height from the toe of the fore-foot, to the pitch of the shoulder twelve foot . . .

— John Josselyn

The moose . . . is appallingly grand as he stands swinging his immense antlers like feathers as he turns to catch a scent in the breeze . . . . The shoulders and broad chest show tremendous strength, and the hips are stout and clean cut; but the great height of a moose is owing chiefly to his long legs and bristling mane . . . . The nose is a marvel of ugliness . . . . The eyes are small and wicked, snapping and gleaming on the slightest provocation, and betray at once the ugly character of their owner.

— Madison Grant

The largest of the American deer . . . heavy and ungainly in appearance, almost grotesque in comparison with the Virginia Deer. The moose is the grandest of all the North American deer. The heavy muzzle, the clumsy body shape, and the somber coloration without relieving touch of contrasting white, certainly are not calculated to win a prize for beauty. There is a suggestion of massive strength and irresistible vigor about a moose that is certain to arouse a feeling of admiration.

— H.E. Anthony

Few animals are more unshapely than this giant deer. His neck slopes down from the shoulder, ending in a head as large as a horse—a head which ends in a nose curled like a camel's . . . . The ears are of enormous length. Yet, ugly as are the nose and ears of the moose, they are his chief means of protection against his enemy, and in that great ungainly head there lurks a brain of marvelous cunning. It is through nose and ears that this cunning brain is duly prompted to escape danger.

— Sir William Francis Butler

Dictionary Definitions: Samuel Johnson, who compiled the first major dictionary of the English language in 1755, defined moose as follows: The large American deer; the biggest of the species of deer.

> *Webster's Dictionary* (1828) provides this definition: "An animal of the genus *Cervus*, and the largest of the deer kind . . . . This animal has palmated horns, with a short thick neck, and the upright mane of a light brown color. The eyes are small, the ears a foot long, very broad, and slouching; the upper lip is square, hangs over the lower one . . . . The animal inhabits cold northern climates . . . . It is the elk of Europe."

> *Webster's Revised Unabridged Dictionary* (1913) provides the following definition: "A large cervine mammal native of the northern United

States and Canada. The adult male is about as large as a horse and has very large palmated antlers. It closely resembles the European elk, and by many zoologists is considered the same species."

The Oxford English Dictionary defines moose as "a cervine animal native to North America closely allied to, or identical with, the European elk."

Etymology of Moose: Etymology is the study of the origins of words. Although some difference of opinion exists on minor points, etymologists agree that the name "moose" is derived from Native Americans. According to a study by the Smithsonian Institute, the word "moose" appears in various Algonquian dialects as follows:

Narragansett and Massachusett: *moos*

Delaware: *mos*

Passamaquoddy: *mus*

Abnake: *monz*

Chippewa: *mons*

Cree: *monswa*

Montagnais: *moosh*

All of these words mean that the moose "eats or strips

off," which is a reference to the way the moose strips bark from a tree to eat it.

Media Moose: When the *New York Times* staff met to discuss a case of journalistic fraud, a stuffed moose was put in the room to encourage staff members to be candid in their discussion. This was a variation of the old idea of the "elephant in the room that no one wants to talk about." It was suggested that staff members "talk to the moose," "deal with the moose," and "put their moose on the table." It was reported that the moose was tossed to anyone asking a tough question. Apparently the moose flew around the room. It is not known if the moose will be nominated for a Pulitzer Prize for his contribution to ethical journalism.

Mis-named Moose: When the first Europeans came to the New World, they made a grievous error. They called the wapiti an elk, which happened to be the name for European moose. Since they called the wapiti an elk, they had no name available for the American animal that should have been called elk; therefore they adopted the Native American name "moose." Thus, what is in Europe an elk is a moose in North America. Or a moose by any other name might still be a moose.

Monsoni: Algonquin language for moose people.

Moose Berry: This is the fruit of the moose bush.

Moose Bird: Once known as the Canada jay, but now called the gray jay (*Perisoreus canadensis*). Since these birds were sometimes seen riding on the antlers of a moose; they were frequently called moose birds. Some report that these birds assist the moose by catching and devouring flies that annoy the moose.

Moose Bush: A shrub found in North America that produces the moose berry.

Moose Call: A trumpet made of birch bark used to call a moose.

Moose Fly: A really big one! Actually moose flies are not all that big, but definitely present a nuisance for moose. Moose fly is the common name given to a species of insect with the scientific name *Haematobosca alcis,* a critter about the size of a housefly.

These flies seem to enjoy biting moose just above the hock, or part way up their hindquarters. Hundreds of flies sometimes swarm over a moose at the same time. Numerous bites of moose flies sometimes cause open, bloody sores on the hind legs of a moose. Fortunately for moose watchers, moose flies do not attack humans.

Moose Gooser: Called the Moose Gooser for reasons that need not be explained, the Alaska Railroad may win the prize for the railroad most closely associated with the moose. After snow accumulates and makes walking difficult, Alaskan moose frequently wander onto the relatively clear railroad tracks, with catastrophic consequences.

To its credit, the Alaska Railroad has tried numerous ways of discouraging moose from walking on the tracks. They have used electrically charged rods jutting out from the front of the locomotive, oscillating red and white lights, signal guns, rockets, wolf scent, low-flying airplanes, and even running a pilot train ahead of the regular train to scare them away. None of these efforts met with much success. But in spite of all the problems the moose have given the Alaska Railroad, conductors on the trains are quick to let passengers know when a moose comes into view. Because of all the moose, perhaps one Native Alaskan called trains the "Iron Moose" instead of the "Iron Horse."

Moose of France: First Nation members—the people living in the Canadian regions of North America when the French came there—had never seen a horse. But they had seen a moose. Therefore, when the French brought the first horses to Quebec in 1655, the natives referred to them as the "Moose of France." They also described a horse pulling a coach as a "rolling cabin drawn by a moose."

Moose Pasture: A Canadian term used to describe a worthless piece of land that can only be used for moose grazing.

Moose Yard: During the winter moose come together and trample down the snow. This winter home for the moose is called a moose yard.

Moosehead Indians: The common name of the Native American Penobscot tribe who lived around Moosehead Lake in Maine.

The Mooseman: Wildlife photographer and writer Bill Silliker Jr., who, prior to teaming up with co-author Walter Griggs for this collection of moose facts, fiction, and trivia, himself penned four books on moose, including his most recent: *Uses for Mooses* (Down East Books) and *Moose Watcher's Handbook* (R.L. Lemke Inc.). Those books—more than any other author on the subject, and perhaps the largest file of moose photographs in the world—earned him the title of The Mooseman. Bill provided the moose photography and most of the biological information in this book, as well as some its moose hysterical content, while leaving most of the serious stuff reported here to the Dean of Moose.

Mooses: Although this word has been used as the plural of moose in book titles (*Uses for Mooses*), songs (*Mooses Come Walking*), and in conversation, it is incorrect English. Also incorrect are such words as meeses, moosi, and meese. An English test might have the following sentence with instructions to circle the correct word: "Frances and Cara saw six (moose, mooses) swimming in the river." Of course the correct answer is moose.

Moosewood: Also known as moose maple or the striped maple. Although this tree has no commercial value, it provides food for the moose; hence the name moosewood.

Moosey: A word coined by Henry David Thoreau in his classic book *The Maine Woods*. Thoreau described the likelihood of encountering a moose when he wrote that the woods were "all mossy and moosey."

Native American Animal Symbols: In Native American culture, each animal represents a different quality of life. The moose was viewed as headstrong, with integrity.

Native American Sign Language: The Native American Sign Language for a moose is as follows: "Bring the hands alongside of head, palms toward it, fingers and thumbs extended, separated, and pointing upwards; move the hands by wrist action to front and rear two or three times, keeping them about parallel to sides of head. This is the sign for the elk. To show the moose, do the elk sign and then holding the left hand still in its position, carry the right in front of and touching it; move right to front, and left to rear, separating hands a few inches." From the book *Indian Sign Language* by W.P. Clark.

Orignac: The name early French explorers gave to the moose, which survives today for French Canadians as *l'orignal.*

Poems: Poets, like prose writers, have focused on the moose in their works and have tried to capture the spirit of the moose in rhyme. Well-known poets wrote some of these poems, while others are by poets who are not well-known or have been largely forgotten.

The following lines have been taken from poems that mention the moose:

The Huron Chief

by Adam Kidd (1802–1831)

I'm the chieftain of this mountain —
  Times and seasons found me here;
My drink has been the crystal fountain,
  My food the wild moose of the deer.

Ode

by Elizabeth Frame (1820–1913)

Upon your ancient hills; your plains
Are laden now with golden grain,
Where carriboo and moose did bound
The railway spans that hunting ground.

Address to a Moose
by Elizabeth Frame (1820–1913)

Hail! Beautiful creature, so stately and bright,
Is danger behind, that thou art in flight;
The chasma of mountains thou clearest at a
      bound,
Thy antlers recumbent, feet spurn the ground.
Why is it that thus thous fliest o'er the vale?
With nostrils expanded thou scentest the gale.
Hail! Lord of the forest. Hail! King of the wood,
Majestic thy form, as listening you stood.

The Arctic Indian's Faith
by Thomas D'Arcy McGee (1825–1868)

Does the Buffalo need the Pale-face word
  To find his pathway far?
What guide has he to the hidden ford,
  Or where the green pastures are?
Who teachest the Moose that the hunter's gun
  Is peering out of the shade?
Who teachest the doe and the fawn to run
  In the track the Moose has made?

The Forest-Ranger's Honeymoon
by Vachel Lindsay (1879–1931)

The moose they say is a whimsical beast.
The pack rat is a curious thing.
Wood wasp, too, is a curious thing.
But a stranger thing was on the wing,
A flying machine, the fire patrol,
Heard from behind a tremendous mountain
Humming on like America's soul.

The Lumberman
by John Greenleaf Whittier (1807–1892)

O'er us, to the southland heading,
Screams the gray wild-goose;
On the night-frost sounds the treading
Of the brindled moose.

The Solitary Woodsman
by Charles G.D. Roberts (1860–1943)

Hear the laughter of the loon
Thrill the dying afternoon,—
Hears the calling of the moose
Each to the early moon.

The Grave Tree
by Bliss William Carmen (1861–1929)

Leave me in the great Lone Country,
For I shall not be afraid
With the shy moose and the beaver
There within my scarlet shade.

To His Lordship

by Charles Albert (Burt) Jones

Deep in the silent forest, where oft I've chanced to
    roam.
The monarch moose inhabits, it is his woodland
    home;
By silent lake at morning, by pond calm at night,
Majestic stands his lordships, stands motionless in
    sight.

The north wind to him is music, the tall pines are his
    friends,
The rivers madly rushing, o'er the rocks and round
    the bends,
Seems to him a heavenly blessing, seems to him the
    work above
Of and kind and thoughtful Father, and His beings
He doth love.

Revenge Will Be Sweet

by Merte H. Craig

Revenge will be sweet to the moose one day,
    As he stalks o'er the land were the North wind
        blows;
When the works of the daring ones fade away,
    And he tramps the graves of his fallen foes.

He will thunder his summons and call for his own.
    And with thousands of hoofs, once again, once
        again;
With never a thought for humanity's mean,
    He will beat down the graves of the children of
        men.

The snow sifting silently all the night long,
    Will crystal each crack, until only a gloam;
Announces the dawn of the dim polar day,
    Where he stables himself in a castaway home.

And each sunless day; as it follows the dawn,
    Of a filtering light thro' the blizzard's wild birth;
Will find the moose quartered with hovering souls,
    Who impassioned by gold, are still shackled to
        earth.

A passion so vast that the wraths of the dead
    Must daily return to the scenes left behind;
There with waiting and longing and fierce racking
        pain
    The whirl of the wheels did there daily grind.

Yes, the hour draws near when the moose will prevail
  Through these valleys and hill he will range as of
          yore;
And the pack-laden human who followed his trail,
  Will vanish; the Klondike will know him no more.

The Laurentides
      by H.R.A. Pocock (1865–1941)

Bright humming-birds flash in the southern sunlight
Of that strange land whose snows surround the Pole;
The Moose, the antler'd Deer, the genial Bear,
Range unprovoked wilds unexplored by man.

Here's to the Land
      by The Rev. William Wye Smith (1827–1917)

Here's to her hills of the moose and the deer;
  Here's to her forest, her fields and her flowers;
Here's to her homes of unchangeable cheer,
  And the maid 'neath the shade of her own native
      bowers!

Birch and Paddle
      by Charles G.D. Roberts (1860–1943)

Have spied the antlered moose

Cropping the young green spruce,

And watched him till betrayed
By the kingfisher's sharp tirade.

Political Moose: The term "bull moose" is used to describe an elite Easterner who goes west to renew his spirit before running for office.

Put the Moose on the Table: The title of the best-selling book by Randall Tobias with Todd Tobias. Randall Tobias, the former CEO of Eli Lilly and Company, provides lessons in leadership. A comment on the scope of the book states "that like a moose in the living room some problems are hard to ignore." In its review of the book, *The Wall Street Journal* suggested that the moose is the current management metaphor.

Quotable Moose: The moose has frequently been used in insightful quotations. Some of these quotations are as follows:

> "Straight as a moose's course."
> > — Old expression found in
> > *Belknap History* 3:120

> "I am as strong as a bull moose."
> > — Theodore Roosevelt, June 27, 1900

"The moose held their convention here last week and have all left town already. I am glad to know they had more manners than the Democrats."

> — Will Rogers in reference
> to the Loyal Order of
> the Moose Convention

"Of all the wonders of nature, a tree in summer is perhaps the most remarkable; with the possible exception of a moose singing 'Embraceable You' in spats."

> — Woody Allen

"Do you want me to put my head in a moose?"

> — Samuel Goldwyn

"A girl needs to prove her love like a moose needs a hat rack."

> — Abigail Van Buren

"There's a moose loose about this plane."

> — Shout on British Airways
> plane in 1994. It
> was really a mouse,
> but the passengers
> shouted "moose."

Slang: Although slang is not acceptable in most circles, it is frequently used. As a slang expression moose can mean:

A physically unattractive person.

A large man or a man with a lip like a moose.

Other uses of the word moose in slang that are more socially acceptable include:

Moose Marshal and Moose Mountie mean game warden.

Moose: A phenomenal-quality coin in coin collecting terminology.

Stump-harsh: The name some early German and Huguenot settlers of Pennsylvania called the moose that they found there. According to naturalist Ernest Thompson Seton, it derived because the moose came into swamps amidst tall black pine stumps to eat lily pads, a staple of a moose's summer diet.

Swamp-donkey: Since a moose looks somewhat like a donkey and likes to feeds in swamps, it has been referred to as a swamp-donkey.

The One About the Farmer's Wife and the Moose: Naturalist Ernest Thompson Seton relates this story about a tame moose adopted from the wild as an orphan by Manitoba farmer Henry Stodgett in his classic work *Lives of Game Animals*, first published in 1909:

It was very affectionate; and when called, would come like a dog; also it was as playful as a kitten, and would, like a kitten, play with a round pebble or croquet ball, striking it with its front feet and running after it. It would gambol with the children, dogs or young cattle. But its playful slaps were no fun for whoever got them, so were not encouraged. Eventually, it became impudent and somewhat dangerous.

In the summer, to escape the flies, it took a notion to come into the kitchen and would lie down on the floor, sprawled all over the place, much to Mrs. Stodgett's indignation. For whacking with a broomstick, it showed utter contempt; and would only budge when it felt like it . . . . Henry was not sorry to pass it on in a horse trade.

Perhaps the moose might have stayed had it had the good sense to mind that broomstick?

Twig Eater: One translation of the Algonquin language for the word moose. Watch a moose munch on the buds and tender ends of tree branches, and you'll agree that it fits.

Legal Moose

Moose have frequently received the attention of the legal system. There has even been a poem entitled "Beasts at Law" by Samuel Woodworth that mentions moose. In addition to this poem there have been actual court cases where the moose has been the subject of the litigation, as well as of laws being passed to protect the moose both from itself and from others.

Perhaps the most critical area of the law involves moose-car collisions. No one wants to kill a moose and no moose is worth the life of a human being. However, a moose should not be held accountable for doing what moose have done since the dawn of time. You cannot train a moose to cross a road, but there are things that can be done to protect the motoring public. For example, New Hampshire has "Brake for Moose" bumper stickers and signs. Other jurisdictions have used fences, reflectors, and lights. Perhaps one day all cars will have devices to warn of on-coming collisions.

Some people believe that hunting laws should be changed in order to eliminate more moose, which would, in turn, reduce the chances of moose-car crashes. Although there is some logic in using WMD (weapons of moose destruction), there must be a better way, since it would be necessary to exterminate the entire moose population to make sure there were no more crashes. Furthermore, although a dead moose will no longer be a traffic hazard, there is no way to show that the moose killed would have been the same moose that might have caused a collision. Hopefully, creativity will prevail over slaughter and cars and moose can coexist safely.

On a much lighter note, perhaps the laws that have been passed to stop a moose from consuming intoxicating beverages are among the most interesting. One can only imagine a moose getting intoxicated at a New Year's Eve party and then trying to walk down the streets of a city. It is not possible to keep four legs doing what four legs are supposed to do if alcohol has polluted the brain. There are more examples of the "legal moose" in this section.

Canada Moose Protection Efforts: An 1865 Canadian Government report addressed the problem of protecting the moose. The report stated that moose poachers were hard to catch because they usually operated at night. The seriousness of the moose's plight was addressed by the government when it stated that "unless legislation can be so made as to reach the offenders and stop the wholesale slaughter, in a few years these useful animals will become extinct." Fortunately for the moose, laws have been passed to protect the moose from extinction.

George the Moose: George is a moose decoy used to catch moose poachers in British Columbia, Canada. George is not an ordinary decoy; he is radio-controlled and has a Styrofoam body covered with moose hide. One can only imagine how a poacher feels when he shoots a decoy moose and ends up paying a fine in excess of $1,000.

Moose Test: Moose and motor vehicles do not mix. Unfortunately, many moose are killed each year when speeding cars meet careless moose. Knowing this, the Swedes have designed the "Moose Test," to determine a car's stability when making a sharp turn to avoid a collision with a moose. A notable casualty of the Moose Test was the Mercedes-Benz A-class, which had to be redesigned after it failed the test.

Moose Warden: Under the 1853 Maine Acts and Resolves, it was declared that "the governor shall . . . appoint one county moose warden for each of the counties."

Signs of the Moose: Moose frequently walk on or beside roads in order to lick the salt left from winter de-icing efforts or to tramp in the nearby "moose muck." Moose have no fear of motor vehicles and when they meet one, it is generally with tragic consequences for driver, moose, and vehicle. In order to prevent such catastrophes, many "moose places" erect signs along the roads warning of moose in the area.

These signs take a number of different forms. One sign features a moose along with the bilingual admonitions to "Slow Down at Night" or "Ralentissez Le Soir." Another graphic sign pictures a bull moose looking askance at a demolished car. New Hampshire's signs have the warning "Brake for Moose" accompanied by a moose silhouette. Scandinavian countries have a triangular warning sign with a walking moose silhouetted in the middle.

Strange Moose Laws: There have been a number of old laws that related to the moose. In Alaska, you cannot watch a moose from an airplane, nor can you push a moose out of an airplane. Reportedly in Fairbanks, Alaska, a moose cannot walk on the sidewalk, nor can it consume alcoholic beverages.

Wrong Way Moose: Douglas Corrigan, a pioneer American aviator, filed a flight plan to fly from New York to California on July 17, 1938. After he took off, he did a 180-degree turn and headed east instead of west. Eventually landing in Ireland, he received a hero's welcome. Corrigan, now known as "Wrong Way," claimed his compass was faulty.

Perhaps some moose also have faulty compasses that guide them to strange places. Moose have frequently strolled through academic institutions, including the University of Massachusetts at Lowell. It was reported that "the moose actually looked in the police chief's office window, but the chief did not see him." Moose have also toured the campuses of the University of Alaska at Fairbanks and Dartmouth College in Hanover, New Hampshire. Perhaps the Dartmouth moose wanted to study business since he visited the Tuck School of Business Administration. It was of Dartmouth that Daniel Webster said, "It is a small college, but there are those who love it." Now Daniel might say, "It was a small moose. And there are those of us who love it!"

Moose have visited government buildings for reasons best known to the moose. A wandering moose almost entered the New Hampshire statehouse in Concord. And a Canadian moose ambled past the guards and went to Rideau Hall to meet the Governor General of Canada. Fortunately the Governor General was not in residence to greet her antlered ambassador. The Royal Canadian Mounted Police, who are known for always "getting their moose," escorted the animal to a wildlife area.

Moose have also visited less exotic places. It was reported that a moose attacked an outhouse, with unfortunate results for the horrified occupant.

Perhaps driven by hunger, a moose wandered into a grocery store in St. John, Newfoundland, Canada, and shopped for more than 24 hours. Apparently a moose lover, the store manager quipped that if "the moose wanted to go shopping, he knew where to go."

Moose have not limited their visits to colleges, statehouses, outhouses, or stores. Moose seem to have an affinity for golf courses. On one occasion, a moose charged out of the nearby woods and strolled down the fairway. Perhaps the woods from where the moose came should be called "Moose Woods." And maybe one day Tiger Woods will hit a ball into the Moose Woods.

 *Military Moose*

The moose is a pacifist. He does not seek out conflict; but when threatened, he becomes nature's battleship. In combat, his giant size makes him seem like a main battle tank, his antlers are like unto sidewinder missiles, and his hooves can attack like a Tomcat jet. It is because of his awesome power and courage that many army and air force units have incorporated the moose into their badges, patches, nose art, and mottoes. Even though the moose is not a seagoing animal, many fighting ships have carried the proud name "moose" on their sterns. In this section there are many examples of how the moose has gone to war with the nations of the world.

Air Force Base: During the Cold War, the United States maintained Loring Air Force Base in Limestone, Maine. This Strategic Air Command base had a sign that prominently displayed a moose looking over the countryside with the phrase "The Moose Is Loose" written under the moose.

The B-52 Stratofortress bombers assigned to this base had a black moose's head with blue eyes superimposed on a map of Maine painted on their tail. And the KC-97 tankers stationed at the base featured a moose's head in red or green to differentiate maintenance squadrons.

Of special note is that flying saucers were spotted over the base on the night of October 7, 1975. Although research is ongoing, it might be that these UFOs were simply moose jumping over the moon.

Air Force Moose: Several air force squadrons and installations adopted the moose as a part of their squadron badges.

The 242nd Squadron of the British Royal Air Force featured a moose's head and the French motto *toujours pr't,* which means "always ready," on its squadron badge. The 242nd Squadron was the first "all Canadian" squadron to serve in the Royal Air Force during World War II. The squadron provided a Canadian presence early in the conflict.

Of special note is its service during the Battle of Britain, when its pilots flew Hurricane fighters and helped win the critical battle for England. The squadron was disbanded in 1964, but it is still remembered. The Battle of Britain Window in the Royal Air Force Chapel in Westminster Abby has the 242nd Squadron badge reproduced in stained glass.

Two other air force squadrons feature a moose on their official badges. The 15th Wing of the Canadian Air Force, based at Moose Jaw, Saskatchewan, has a moose on its squadron badge with the words "Serving the Future" inscribed under the moose. This base serves as the home of the Snowbirds, Canada's world-famous aerobatic team.

The United States Air Force has one squadron with a moose logo. The 503rd Bombardment Squadron was active in World War II, when it served as a replacement training squadron. It flew both the B-17 Flying Fortress and B-24 Liberator. The squadron's emblem prominently features a moose with two aerial bombs in the background.

Walt Disney Studios designed many patches for air force units during World War II. The Royal Canadian Air Force Wireless Station at Patricia Bay, British Columbia, had a Disney moose with radio signals flashing behind him.

Two United States Air Force units also used moose patches provided by the Disney Studios. The 3rd Air Force featured a flying moose with bombs in its antlers and the 450th Bombardment Squadron had a crouching moose with boxing gloves. The moose on these patches were not "Mickey Mouse" moose. They were defiant moose that lowered their antlers in defense of freedom.

Airplane Moose: In addition to their squadron emblems, both official and unofficial, aircrews frequently have painted distinctive nose art on their planes. Some examples:

> *Big Moose* was the name of a B-17. Flying to Europe in 1943, *Big Moose* got off course and ditched in the Atlantic Ocean. Fortunately, most of the crew survived, but *Big Moose* disappeared into the ocean depths. Fifty years later, an

Icelandic fisherman caught a part of *Big Moose*. Eventually, a portion of the plane was brought to the surface. The moral of the story is that you cannot keep a Big Moose down.

Bullwinkle graces the nose of BLAYAK, a Russian-built Yak-11 now used to air race in the United States. Since the aircraft type was known by the NATO code name Moose, it seemed appropriate that its racing owner paint a picture of Bullwinkle with the acronym BLAYAK over it. BLAYAK is a combination of the color of the aircraft (black) and Yak, the type of aircraft.

Dynamic Duo, (Rocky and Bullwinkle) F-105D Thunderchief, 192nd Tactical Fighter Group

Dynamic Duo II, (Rocky and Bullwinkle) F-105D Thunderchief, 192nd Tactical Fighter Group

The Flyin' Moose, B-24J Liberator, 491st Bomb Group (lost in action November 26, 1944)

Moose, B-26B Marauder, 451st Bomber Squadron

Moose, P-51D Mustang fighter, 357th Fighter Group

Moose. A picture of a moose was painted on the nose of the 1000th Canadian-built Lancaster bomber.

Moose. A picture of a moose was painted on the nose of an RAF Spitfire MK IIA.

Moose after Hitler, Halifax Bomber, 419th (Moose) Squadron, RCAF

Moose Jaw, D.H. Mosquito 98

Red Moose Express, B-17E, Flying Fortress, 43rd Bomber Group

The Moose Is Loose, B-29 Super Fortress, 504th Bomb Group (crashed on its 7th mission returning to Tinian on June 7, 1945)

The Moose Is Loose, KC-135 Stratotanker, 42nd Air Refueling Squadron

Moose Nose, P51-D 368th Fighter Squadron

Spruce Moose, C-130E (Operation Desert Shield)

The Wild Moose, C-119 C, Flying Boxcar, 61st Troop Carrier Squadron

Bull Moose Battalion: During World War I, the 141st Canadian Battalion was known as the Bull Moose Battalion. When many of its members were transferred to the 52nd Canadian Battalion, the 52nd assumed the Bull Moose name. The unit used this name because many of the soldiers were "moose-like" in size and ate moose meat.

Civil War Moose: Moose made their appearance at a

number of significant battles of the Civil War—adorning flags:

> The moose is featured on the great seal of the State of Maine. During the Civil War, the 16th Maine Volunteer Infantry carried a regimental flag with this seal on it. As this flag flew over many battlefields, it's likely that some of the Confederate soldiers saw their first moose emblazoned on this flag. Today this flag is preserved in the Maine State Museum.

> The flag of the United States 1st Michigan Infantry Regiment featured both a moose and an elk, which represent Michigan. Confederate forces captured the flag at the battle of First Manassas, and it was not returned to the State of Michigan until 1886. The flag is now on display in the Michigan State Capitol building.

Frequent Flyer Moose: Moose have dignified two aircraft with their namesake. The Russian two-seat basic trainer, the Yak-11, carries the NATO designation Moose. (The Warsaw Pact called it the "Hawk"). The use of the name, moose, makes for quick identification and avoids confusion, which can come from mispronouncing Yakovley Yak-11. The aircraft, which entered service in 1947 as an advanced trainer, has now been retired from service.

The United States Air Force uses a cargo and troop transport plane of more recent vintage, the C-17 Globemaster III. Because of its large size, antler-like winglets, and the "venting sound it makes during fueling" that sounds like a moose mating call, the plane is frequently referred to as "the Moose."

Homer the Moose: Homer is a sailor aboard the United States Coast Guard Cutter *Hickory* (WLB 212), home-ported in Homer, Alaska. Homer's job is to act as a tour guide and help the members of the Coast Guard to continue being the "Guardians of the Seas."

Infantry Regiments: The moose has a special relationship to ground forces. The Swedes actually used the moose as a cavalry mount. Although the Swedes were able to ride the moose, the moose would retreat when a battle started.

In spite of its pacifist nature, several Canadian infantry regiments featured the moose on their hat badges. The Algonquin Regiment served in both World Wars. Its badge featured the head of a bull moose with the words *kee she nah*. These Ojibway words mean "we surpass" or "we conquer."

Other Canadian infantry units that featured a moose on their badges include:

The Sault Ste. Marie and Sudbury Regiment

Moose Jaw / 128th Overseas Battalion

New Brunswick Rangers

Military Vehicle: While serving in Kosovo, a Swedish Armored Personnel Carrier (Pbv 302) had four miniature stickers featuring moose under a painting of the Swedish flag. (The moose stickers probably represented kills by the crew of the vehicle.)

Moose Armor: Gustavus Adolphus the Great, the King of Sweden from 1611 to 1632 and the defender of Protestant lands in Germany, was killed at the Battle of Lutzen in 1632. Generally, body armor was made of metal plates covered with cloth or leather; however, Gustavus Adolphus was wearing armor of elk [moose] skin and the skin failed to stop a bullet. If nothing else, the lesson is clear that moose skin works best on a moose and should not be relied upon as body armor.

Moose Squadron: The 419th Squadron of the Royal Canadian Air Force. Known as the Moose Squadron in honor of its first commanding officer, John "Moose" Fulton, the Moose Squadron achieved its greatest fame flying Lancaster bombers on night raids over Germany during World War II.

King George VI of England, who presented the squadron its official badge, recognized the squadron's accomplishments. The badge displays a moose with head lowered to attack. Beneath the moose is the squadron's motto *Moosa aswayita,* which in Cree means "Beware of the Moose." A stained-glass window at the Royal Air Force Base at Mildenhall, England, honors the service of this squadron. The charging moose of the 419th Squadron appears above a quotation from Thomas Payne: "These are the times that try men's souls."

The most distinguished member of the Moose Squadron was Pilot Officer Andrew Mynarski, who was the mid-upper gunner of a Lancaster bomber. On the night of June 12, 1944, Mynarski's aircraft was attacked from below by a German fighter and burst into flames. Pilot Officer Mynarski was ordered to bail out, and could have with the rest of the crew, but he noticed that the rear turret gunner was trapped in his turret. Mynarski "made his way through the flames in an effort to break open the rear turret and save the trapped gunner." While so doing, his parachute and clothing were engulfed in flames. He could not get the rear turret open and then, obeying the request of the trapped gunner, he turned to leave. As a last gesture "he turned towards him [the trapped gunner], stood at attention in his flaming clothing, and saluted before he jumped out of the plane." Although Mynarski died, Pat Brophy, the rear gunner, survived the crash of the Lancaster bomber. Brophy later said, "I will always believe that a divine providence intervened to save me because of what I had seen, so that the world might know of a gallant man who laid down his life for a friend." For his courage and sacrifice, Pilot Officer Andrew Mynarski was awarded the Victoria Cross, the British Commonwealth's highest award for valor. The famed Moose Squadron has no greater hero than Andrew Mynarski.

Moose Squadron Mascots: Herman the Moose, a mounted moose head, served with the 419th Squadron of the Royal Canadian Air Force during World War II. Following the war, Herman returned with the squadron to Canada in a Lancaster bomber. Herman was officially retired in 1955 and replaced by Bruce.

Officially, Bruce was known as Bruce MKI. When the squadron was ordered overseas, Bruce MKI remained in Canada and was replaced by Bruce MKII.

In 1962, when the squadron was deactivated, the squadron members toasted their first commander, John "Moose" Fulton, with the words, "We have tried to honour you, Sir, in the only way we could—by making the Moose Squadron the best of its kind anywhere. We know we did not fail you."

Bruce MKII was declared dead and was buried with full military honors. The last entry in the squadron's log was "RIP Bruce: who owns the Rhine." Bruce MKI, the mascot still in Canada, was retired with the belief that he would soon be called to active duty.

When the squadron was reactivated in 1975, Bruce MKI reported for duty. The squadron was again deactivated for a time, but was reactivated on July 28, 2000, as a training squadron. This was the fourth reactivation of the squadron, which suggests that you cannot keep a good moose down on the ground. As a squadron historian wrote: "The legend of the moose lives on."

Royal Canadian Moose: The 604th Squadron of the Royal Canadian Air Cadets is known as the Moose Squadron. This organization provides training for young people interested in aviation.

Sea-Going Moose: The moose is a powerful swimmer and water is one of its favorite habitats. The Germans, who sometimes call them marsh stags, recognize the close association of the moose with water. Therefore, it is not surprising that the name moose has been assigned to several Canadian and United States warships dating back a long time. Perhaps the first of these was *L'Original* (The Moose). Described as the King's Ship, it sank at Quebec, Canada, while being launched in 1750. An 1898 report stated that the cause of the disaster "was due to the mistakes of the builder."

Other Canadian ships include:

> HMCS *Moose* was an armed yacht that served in World War II. Launched in 1930, she was originally named *Cleopatra*. The ship was renamed *Moose* in 1940 and served the Canadian Navy until 1945. Perhaps only the Canadians would prefer a moose to a Cleopatra.

> HMCS *Moose* (ML111) was a Canadian 112-foot "B" Class motor launch. ML111 was renamed *Moose* in 1954 as a reminder of the armed yacht *Moose*, whose duty she assumed following the end of World War II. The ship's badge

displays "a moose standing in water in an attitude of watchfulness."

HMCS *Moose Jaw* (K160) was a Flower Class corvette (coastal escort vessel) that served in the Canadian Navy from 1941 until 1945. This ship rammed and aided in the sinking of U-501 in September 1941. Perhaps, it could be said that the moose put its jaws around the U-Boat and the U-Boat was "kaput."

The United States Navy has named several ships Moose.

The first USS *Moose* was a stern wheel gunboat that served in the Union Navy during the Civil War. She was decommissioned at the end of the war.

The second USS *Moose* (IX-24) was commissioned as a ship of the United States Navy on January 28, 1944. Assigned to the South Pacific, she served as an oil-storage and fuel-supply ship. She was decommissioned at the end of the war and became known as the *Mason L. Weems*. She was subsequently renamed the *Yankee Pioneer* and then the *Y. L. McCormick*. Although much renamed, a moose by any other name is still a moose.

The United States Navy's first USS *Moosehead* was a patrol boat that served in World War I.

The second USS *Moosehead* (IX 98) carried passengers, mail, and cargo during World War II.

The *Moose Peak* was a V-4 tug that helped tow the artificial harbors across the English Channel. These harbors, known as Mulberries, made the Normandy invasion possible. The *Moose Peak* almost suffered a disaster when a German U-Boat surfaced close to it, but did it no harm.

The USS *Moosbrugger* (DD980) was a Spruance-class destroyer that served in the United States Navy from 1976 until 2000. The ship was named in honor of Rear Admiral Frederick Moosbrugger, who was awarded the Navy Cross for his action during the World War II Naval Battle of Vella Gulf in the South Pacific. Although the destroyer was named in his honor, it was known to its crew as the "Moose." The ship had a set of moose antlers mounted below the bridge and a moose painted on the radio room door. It served with distinction in the Gulf War. The ship was described as "head and antlers" above the rest. When at sea, it was said that the "Moose is loose."

Although not named for a moose, three United States Navy ships have moose associations:

During World War II, the USS *Norton Sound* (AV 11) had a moose emblem drawn by the Disney Studios. The badge features a moose standing on top of a seaplane while repairing it.

The USS *Maine* (BB10) was one of the most famous ships in American history. The USS *Maine* sailed to Havana in an effort to force Spain to grant Cuba independence. On the night of February 15, 1898, the *Maine* exploded with great loss of life. "Remember the Maine" became a battle cry and the United States was soon at war with Spain. One of the casualties of the loss of the USS *Maine* was the silver loving cup with moose-antler handles that was presented by the city of New Orleans to the USS *Maine* in 1897.

The USS *Theodore Roosevelt* (CVN 71) is a United States aircraft carrier. Since President Theodore Roosevelt was known as "the Bull Moose," it is not surprising that his namesake carrier has a moose mascot. The Roosevelt foundation donated a stuffed moose head that is kept in a case on the hangar bay. There is also Sagamore T. Moose, who is called "Bully." Bully's costume is described as "a big fur outfit with a big head." Because of the close clearances on an aircraft carrier, Bully's antlers are smaller than normal. For friend or foe, Sagamore T. Moose symbolizes the determination of the United States to "sail quietly and carry a big moose."

Tank Transporter: The Israeli Army used a Mack truck as a tank transporter. The truck was equipped with a front made out of diamond-plate steel. This addition was referred to as a "moose killer."

 *Nationalistic Moose*

The moose is a highly respected animal and is frequently displayed as a symbol of national pride in both the United States and Canada. These moose-loving nations have placed the moose on their stamps, license plates, currency, state and tribal flags, as well as municipal seals. Alaska and Maine have named the moose as their state animal. But national moose pride is not limited to the Western Hemisphere.

Several European nations have also pictured the moose on their currency, stamps, and local flags. Norway has adopted the moose as its national animal and the moose is considered the unofficial animal of Sweden. Most nations that have moose among their animals have recognized them in special ways. This section will provide additional examples of the nationalistic moose.

Flags and Seals: Several American states and Canadian provinces proudly display the moose on their official seals and flags.

> The State of Maine features a recumbent moose in front of a pine tree on its state seal and flag.

The State of Michigan displays an elk and a moose on its state seal and flag.

The Coat of Arms of the Province of Ontario has a moose on it.

The crest of the Town of Fort Frances, Ontario, Canada, features a bull moose, maple leaves, two men in a canoe, a white pine tree, and a magneto. There is something intriguing about a magneto, which represents electricity, and a moose, which represents wildlife, appearing on the same crest. Since the moose seems to be standing on the magneto, it suggests that the moose might be electrified.

Money: In 1983 Canada issued a National Parks silver dollar to commemorate the founding of its national park system. The coin depicted a Canadian moose against a backdrop of the Rocky Mountains. In 1996 Canada issued a fifty-cent sterling-silver proof coin that featured a moose calf. Many other nations have featured the moose on their coins and currency, including Belarus, which displays a moose on its 25-ruble note.

Stamps: The moose has been featured on many postage stamps. Sweden pictured the moose on its first triangular stamps. The United States and Canada have also featured the moose on postage stamps. On December 19, 2003

Canada Post released a $5 stamp. The moose on this stamp displays a full spread of antlers. Truly, it's a magnificent moose displayed on a beautiful stamp, eh!

In addition to postage stamps, there have been a number of instances of moose being featured on other stamps. In 1999, New Hampshire pictured the moose on its new habitat stamp.

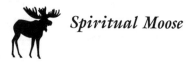 *Spiritual Moose*

Native Americans revered the moose and included it in their tribal stories. One example is the legend recorded by Henry David Thoreau, which claimed that the moose came from whales. Another myth suggests that the moose aided in the creation of the Rocky Mountains. Still another tale explains why the moose has a hump on its back.

This section will provide examples of how different cultures have included the moose in their spiritual traditions and how these traditions have provided a different perspective on our understanding of the moose.

Bullrock, the Moose: In Dixfield, Maine, there is a life-size carving of Bullrock, the moose. Carved by Ted Walker, using a chainsaw, Bullrock is remembered for his unfortunate death. Under the carving there is a stone with the following inscription:

> Bullrock, the Dixfield Moose, is named in memory of a moose of local legend. According to the legend, a wandering moose journeyed from the back side of Dixfield's Sugarloaf Mountain. As he approached the rock formation now known as "Bullrock," he became so entranced with the beauty of the valley below that he lost his footing and plunged over the edge. Today Bullrock's spirit can be seen in the majesty of our forests and in the steadfastness of our people. He not only symbolizes Dixfield's colorful past, but represents a strong and steady future for all of us.

Catfish: A Native American myth tells how a school of militant catfish tried to kill a moose. In the ensuing confrontation, the moose trampled to death all of the catfish that were unable to slither to safety. Want proof? The catfish still have their spears, but they also have flat heads from being stomped by the moose. The moral to this story is: Don't mess with a moose unless you want a flat head.

Dreams of Moose: A Native American legend states that if you dreamed of moose you would have a long life. Maybe people should count moose instead of counting sheep and enjoy a long life.

Hydrated Moose: A Native American legend tells of a

moose drinking all the water from a river. To keep the river from running dry and causing the other animals to die of thirst, a fly attacked the gulping moose. Unable to swat the fly, the moose stopped drinking and retreated into the forest. This old legend has a basis in fact, since the moose fly continues to be a nemesis for the moose.

Moose Mythology: The Iroquois refer to the blowing of the east wind as "the moose spreading his breath."

Moose Tale: Henry David Thoreau told of an old Native American legend that claimed a whale came out of the ocean, became dehydrated, and evolved into a moose. Although this might seem like a big fish story, it does explain not only how the moose got so large, but also why it still likes the water.

Moses and the Moose: Ernest Thompson Seton, naturalist and co-founder of the Boy Scouts of America, in his book *The Ten Commandments of the Animal World,* suggested that the Ten Commandments apply not only to humans but to all highly developed animals. Like the Native Americans, Seton found a spiritual meaning in the moose.

Seton told the story of a seriously wounded moose chasing a mailman up a tree. Although the moose could have killed the mailman, he just looked at him and did him no harm. After a time, the moose collapsed and died. Seton suggests that "when animals are in terrible trouble, when they have done all that they can do, and are face-to-face with despair and death, there is then revealed in them an instinct that prompts them to throw themselves on the mercy of some other power not knowing whether it be friendly or not, but very sure that it is superior." Seton continued his thesis by suggesting that humans, when in distress, reach for the heavenly light of God.

Noah's Moose: Sages do not have to ponder over whether or not there were moose on Noah's Ark. Obviously there were, as we still have moose. But there is more to the story of the Ark than saving moose. Of all of the stories of the ancient world, none rival the story of Noah and his Ark in popularity. The thought of all of the world's animals loaded on a boat and sailing for forty days and forty nights creates a fantastic mental picture.

The ancient Jews and others have embellished this story. Reportedly, there was an animal called the "reem" that was so big it could not get on board the Ark, so it was tied behind the Ark. The giant "og" was lashed to the roof of the Ark. And there is the story of the unicorn, which was left behind because it was playing while the moose were being loaded. Now, what about the moose? In order to fill an unfortunate gap in Noah's story, a new legend needs to be created.

It seems that two moose were walking on the deck of the Ark during an especially violent thunderstorm. The bull moose was using his massive antlers as lighting rods, while the cow moose was using her powerful voice as a foghorn. As the two moose walked about, their long tails were trailing behind them. Suddenly, a wave hit the Ark and Noah was thrown overboard. Several birds quickly flew off to rescue him, but they could not lift him out of the turbulent water. Then a shark raced toward Noah. Its mouth was wide open as it anticipated having Noah for lunch. Courageously, the two moose ran to the edge of the ark and dangled their long tails over the side.

Noah grabbed the two moose tails and pulled himself back on the Ark. He was saved! Unfortunately, the enraged shark bit off the tails of the two moose. Now virtually tailless, the moose were heroes to all of the other animals. Suddenly, the earth quivered, the winds roared, the thunder rolled, the lightening flashed, and God said, "Brother and sister moose, you have saved my servant Noah. Henceforth, your tails will always be short to remind everyone of your selfless act that saved Noah and his chosen people." Of course, this is just a legend. Or is it?

Pamola: Pamola is the name of a creature in Penobscot mythology that lives on Mount Katahdin in Maine. Pamola has been generally described as having the head and antlers of a moose, the wings of a bird, the body of a man, and the beak and legs of an eagle. Henry David Thoreau wrote that "Pamola is always angry with those who climb its mountain." While no one has been able to photograph the mythical Pamola, one of the peaks of Katahdin bears this Native American spirit's name.

Praying Moose: The insect kingdom has the praying mantis. Does the animal kingdom have the praying moose? Consider that when a moose drinks water from a puddle or licks salt from a road surface, it kneels down as if in prayer. The sight of a genuflecting moose suggests that the moose is grateful for the sustenance it has been provided.

Religious Moose: Many Native Americans and First Nation Bands referred to the moose in their religious observances. Egerton Ryerson Young, a Methodist missionary in the last years of the nineteenth century, recorded the following reflections by a member of the Nelson River Indians in Canada: "I hear God in the thunder, in the tempest, and in the storm; I see His power in the lightning that shivers the tree into kindling wood; I see His goodness in giving us the moose, the reindeer, the beaver, and the bear; I see His loving kindness in giving us, when the south winds blow, the ducks and geese; and when the snow and ice melt away, and our lakes and rivers are open again, I see how he fills them with fish. I have watched these things for years, and I see how during every moon of the year He gives us something . . . ."

Spiritual Moose: The Native American and First Nation members held the moose in high regard. This respect was demonstrated by the way they treated a deceased moose. Since the moose was able to hear people talk about him, his ears were removed and buried at his death. And unused parts of a moose were hung in a tree as a sign of respect and to encourage the moose to return to the land. Out of respect, the skull of a moose was not used as a trophy.

Squashed Moose: A Native American legend suggests that, when first created, moose were large animals that towered above everything. They took advantage of their great size and intimidated the other animals. Concerned about the moose's arrogance, the Great Spirit squeezed them down to their present size, which gave the moose its humped back, puffy nose, and ungainly appearance.

 *Biblio-Moose*

Material for this book was collected over several decades. The four primary sources were *The Ecology and Management of the North American Moose* compiled and edited by Albert W. Franzmann and Charles C. Schwartz, *North American Moose* by Randolph L. Peterson, *The Moose Book* by Samuel Merrill, and *Habits, Haunts and Anecdotes of the Moose* by Charles Albert (Burt) Jones.

Some photographs and visual material courtesy of the New Hampshire Fish and Game Department, Calgary E.M.G., Jay Paul, Frontier Airlines, Moosehead Breweries, Ltd., and David Kenyon.

Other valuable information and assistance was obtained from the following sources: interviews, newspapers, magazines, the Outdoor Channel, Michigan Department of Natural Resources, the World Wide Web, the United States Navy, *National Geographic*, Moose International, the *Moose Call,* the North American Moose Foundation, Mayor Mel Lastman of Toronto, Canada, Darryl Allen, Jill Kramer, Linda Pontius, Nancy and Peter D'Alema, Peggy Bullinger,

Mary Johns, Bob and Sue Griggs, the United States Air Force, the Artscape Program of Pittsfield, Massachusetts, the University of Montana, the Hudson's Bay Company, the United States Customs Service, Dr. Vince Crichton, Jeanne Scott, Dr. and Mrs. Charles Blem, Ray McAllister, the Royal Canadian Air Force, Early Canadiana Online, the Library and Archives of Canada, the Alaska State Library, the Crown Copyright Office, and herds of moose lovers from Algonquin Park, Ontario, to Richmond, Virginia.

 *Moose Mail*

If you enjoyed this book and would like to contribute to future editions, please send your ideas, photos, and suggestions to me at the following address:

>Dr. Walter S. Griggs Jr.
>School of Business
>Virginia Commonwealth University
>Box 4000
>1015 Floyd Ave.
>Richmond, VA 23284-4000

Thank you,

Walter